NUMBER TWENTY
The Walter Prescott Webb Memorial Lectures

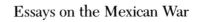

Essays on the Mexican War

[THE WALTER PRESCOTT WEBB MEMORIAL LECTURES]

Essays on the Mexican War

By WAYNE CUTLER, JOHN S. D. EISENHOWER,
MIGUEL E. SOTO, DOUGLAS W. RICHMOND

Introduction by ARCHIBALD HANNA
Edited by DOUGLAS W. RICHMOND

Published for the University of Texas at Arlington by
Texas A&M University Press: College Station

Library of Congress Cataloging-in-Publication Data

Essays on the Mexican War.

(The Walter Prescott Webb memorial lectures; no. 20)
Includes bibliographies.
1. United States—History—War with Mexico, 1845–1848.   I. Cutler, Wayne,
1938–   II. Richmond, Douglas W., 1946–   III. University of Texas at
Arlington.   IV. Series: Walter Prescott Webb memorial lectures; 20.
E404.E87   1986   973.6′2   86-5886
ISBN 0-89096-291-X

Manufactured in the United States of America
FIRST EDITION

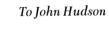

To John Hudson

Contents

Illustrations

Preface

ON March 14, 1985, the University of Texas at Arlington hosted the twentieth annual Walter Prescott Webb Memorial Lectures. More people than usual attended the lectures. Because the state of Texas was preparing to celebrate the sesquicentennial of its independence, a topic such as the 1846–48 war between Mexico and the United States had special significance. The war not only served to cement the 1845 annexation of Texas into the United States but it aroused bitter feelings in Mexico that remain today.

The subjects chosen and speakers presenting them were much closer to Webb's primary field of interest than any past gathering had been. The essays in this volume present new hypotheses concerning the war and shed light on previously dark areas. The Mexican War remains a fresh field for research, and the authors have done much to satisfy the need for new interpretations.

The efforts of Will Holmes, the late Harold Hollingsworth, and E. C. Barksdale, the former chair of history at the University of Texas at Arlington, led to the inauguration of the Webb Lectures series in 1965. Under the leadership of Richard G. Miller, the successor to Barksdale as department chair, the lectures grew in stature. Stanley Palmer, current chair, strives to see that the lectures continue to gain in reputation.

Several people deserve to be acknowledged for their timely contributions. C. B. Smith, Sr., of Austin has underwritten the publication of the Webb Lectures. A former student of Professor Webb and a baseball player at the University of Texas at Arlington when it was Grubbs Vocational College, C. B. Smith has provided indispensable support to the lecture and publication program. Jenkins and Virginia Garrett have helped establish the library's Division of Special Collections, where some of the authors researched their topics. Central to

Special Collections is the extensive collection of rare books, graphics, manuscripts, newspapers, and microfilm contained in the Jenkins Garrett Library, which also maintains one of the nation's most comprehensive collection of books and documents on the Mexican War. Mention should also be made of Sandra Myres, who chairs the Webb Lectures Committee and has moved the program in an increasingly professional direction.

Closer to home, I must acknowledge the kindness of Shirley Rodnitzky, who facilitated the use of many documents from Special Collections. As director of the Texas Humanities Library, Frances Leonard provided many of the illustrations used in this volume. Olga Esskandanian and Sarah Brannon typed the essays with care.

Finally, something should be said about the person to whom this book is dedicated. John Hudson came to UT Arlington in 1957 and transformed the library from a small, junior college operation into one that was more than respectable. In addition to a fine Cartographic History Library and the Texas Labor Archives, Hudson was particularly concerned about Latin American studies. He took great interest in establishing the library's Yucatán Collection, which ultimately amounted to 1,078 rolls of microfilm made from one and a half million pages of religious, governmental, and newspaper documents. Always gifted with an instinct for finding money, Hudson and Sandra Myres obtained grants to film the material in 1972, a project that continued for six years. Hudson subsequently began filming Honduran and Costa Rican archives during his final years.

Sadly, the sound of Hudson's high-pitched laughter ended on May 23, 1984, when he died in Cancún after being hospitalized for an intestinal infection. His smile and availability have left a void on this campus. John's keen intellect and broad realm of knowledge will be remembered. His chief concern seemed to emanate from a firm desire to bring together patrons and library holdings for scholarly discourse. His sharp wit and unusual vision caused his colleagues to reflect more seriously upon their work.

DOUGLAS W. RICHMOND

Essays on the Mexican War

Introduction

AMID the confusion and triumph of the closing days of World War II, the centenary of the war between the United States and Mexico passed largely unnoticed in this country, though not in Mexico. The 1950s had its own war in Korea to think of. The 1960s, proclaiming peace and the irrelevance of war, observed the centennial of the Civil War by either criticizing the loss of life or arguing about the treatment of slaves. Certainly the Civil War Centennial aroused more interest among historians than among the general public. But beginning in the 1970s there has been a renewed interest in this first of our wars to be fought on foreign soil. Not only has Justin Smith's history, for decades the standard secondary work on the subject and for years out of print, been reissued, but also a number of the classic personal narratives written by participants have appeared. Other contemporary sources have been brought to light and into print. The interest of collectors and consequently of booksellers in the Western Americana field has been drawn to this area, and important collections of source material such as the Jenkins Garrett Collection, now at the University of Texas at Arlington, and the Frederick W. Beinecke Collection at Yale have been made available to scholars. The result has been a modest but steady flow of serious historical monographs on a wide variety of aspects of the war.

There are a number of reasons why historians had so long neglected this phase of American history. As wars go, the Mexican War was a minor one, of comparatively short duration and involving relatively small numbers of troops on either side. Military history, like local history, has usually been considered by the profession to be a minor field, of interest chiefly to the amateurs and antiquarians. Major historians who dealt with the Mexican War tended to treat it simply as one more detail in the large picture of westward expansion and Manifest Destiny.

There has been a certain moral uneasiness about the origins of this war. Americans, like the citizens of other nations, will support wholeheartedly only those wars they consider to be just. Although the majority of the nation was undoubtedly suffused with patriotic fervor in 1845, there was a large and extremely vocal minority that saw the war only as an attempt to extend the system of slavery at the expense of a weak and helpless neighbor. Though minority protests could not prevent the war, they were remembered long after slavery had been abolished and the ardor of Manifest Destiny had cooled. Even in this century there has been a certain reluctance to probe old wounds at the risk of damaging already fragile relations with Mexico.

Nevertheless, it now seems possible and indeed desirable for historians to reexamine traditional concepts of the Mexican War and also to explore hitherto neglected questions. This topic is particularly appropriate for the twentieth annual Walter Prescott Webb lectures because of the crucial role of Texas in that conflict and the presence at Arlington of the Jenkins Garrett Collection.

When Karl von Clausewitz in his *Art of War* made the oft-quoted pronouncement "War is only the continuation of politics by other means," he was referring to the dynastic power struggles of late eighteenth- and early nineteenth-century Europe. But the war between the United States and Mexico exemplifies his maxim in quite a different sense. The genesis of the war may have owed as much to the internal political situation in both nations as to the existence of any international grievances insoluble by normal diplomatic procedures. Similarly, the measures adopted for the conduct of the war were as often determined by domestic political considerations as by sound military strategy.

Miguel Soto's essay, "The Monarchist Conspiracy and the Mexican War," is a lucid and carefully researched account of a little-known episode in Mexican political history—an attempt in 1845 to subvert the Mexican republic and establish a monarchy with a Spanish prince at its head. For the conspiracy to be successful it was necessary for General Paredes y Arrillaga to retain control of the army. But in order to maintain his position, the general was forced to be even more bellicose than his rivals. For ten years a succession of Mexican leaders had used the Texan revolt and the bogeyman of North American invasion to justify revolt, dictatorship, and financial exactions. To speak of peace meant political suicide. A parallel may be seen in the fate of those American politicians who in recent decades were accused of being soft on communism. Paredes was forced to support a war that could only end in ruining his own career and any hopes for a monarchy.

If the political situation in the United States was not as chaotic as that in Mexico, it was nonetheless subject to tension and discord. Though half a century older than its neighbor to the south and far more homogenous ethnically and economically, the northern republic was still a long way from the unity its title proclaimed. Sectional rivalry was being aggravated and embittered by agitation of the slavery question. It was the struggle against a common enemy that had made reluctant allies of the thirteen original states, and even that measure of unity had been imperiled in the War of 1812. It is fear that Wayne Cutler sees behind Polk's efforts for the Union thirty years later and his expansionism as well—not fear of a foreign enemy but fear of a consolidation of wealth and power. For Polk in 1845 as for Jefferson in the Louisiana Purchase, the aim was not imperial power but such a dispersion of economic and political strength as to make a centralized tyranny impossible. If we accept this thesis, we must consider the fact that although the antislavery advocates were the most vocal opponents of the war, the most influential opponents would have been those members of the eastern establishment who opposed territorial expansion because it would inevitably dilute their economic and political influence.

Cutler's paper, "President Polk's New England Tour: North for Union," does not belabor these theoretical questions. It is, rather, a fascinating picture of the ceremonial exercise of the presidency at a period when both transportation and communications were just beginning the transition from the horse to steam and electricity. We have become accustomed in our own time to the radio fireside chat, the televised news conference, the press release, and videotapes. Polk's world was far different, but the basic principles of showmanship and political skills were the same. Cutler has given us an intriguing exposition of their detailed application more than a century ago.

John Eisenhower has explored still another aspect of the politics of war—the relationship between the president as commander in chief and his generals in the field. This is a part of the larger question of the relationship between the armed forces and the civil government. We in this country take it for granted that the supreme command of the military always rests in civilian hands. Indeed, it is hard to see how a democracy could continue to exist otherwise. But in much of the world that situation does not exist and never has.

Along with the abhorrence of centralized power that, according to Cutler, President Polk inherited from Jefferson and the founding fathers from their British ancestors, was an equally strong distrust of standing armies. Yet from the day of their founding, the colonies were forced to make provision for their own defense against a variety of enemies. Of the little more than 150 years before the American Revolution, 50 were war years, whether local conflicts with Indians or extensions of European war. To provide the necessary forces the Americans developed a militia system based on the English train bands of Cromwell's day. The system was never satisfactory from a strictly military point of view, but in one form or another it provided the bulk of our armies down to the opening days of World War II, and still exists today in the National Guard. In spite of repeated demonstrations of its disastrous inefficiency, the minuteman legend, the concept of the citizen-soldier springing to arms at a moment's notice, persisted.

The Mexican War, Eisenhower states, was the turning point. The regular army, augmented by regiments of volunteer enlistees, fought and won the battles. Hastily mobilized militia units played a minor role. For the first time, the regular army officers, graduates of the still-distrusted Military Academy, demonstrated their professional competence and won the respect of the nation.

Along with the distrust of a standing army went the easy assumption that political leadership was instantly convertible to military command. The top commands did remain with the regular army in the persons of Winfield Scott and Zachary Taylor in spite of Polk's strong desire to name Senator Thomas Hart Benton. The effect of political influence in the naming of their subordinates was revealed in the squabble over credit for the victory after Scott's successful campaign to Mexico City. It is a fact of American politics that although members of the armed forces are forbidden to seek elective office, a candidate's war record can become almost a prerequisite for election.

It will be noted that of the four papers composing this year's volume, only the Trussell letters deal with military history in the traditional sense, and even they are somewhat peripheral since his regiment, the 2nd Mississippi Riflemen, arrived in Mexico too late to take part in combat. Nevertheless, their inclusion is most appropriate since they provide contemporary documentation for the strained relations between volunteers and regular army discussed by Eisenhower as well as comments on politics in both the United States and Mexico that are germane to Cutler's and Soto's papers.

These then are some of the questions explored in the Webb Lectures this year. It is to be hoped that they will stimulate further interest along these lines and also suggest other areas of investigation.

President Polk's New England Tour: North for Union

WHEN Polk's efforts for Union are juxtaposed with his better known politics of expansion, there is a tendency to assume that the two policies are inconsistent and incompatible. Yet the apparent logic of such an assumption fails if correct historical antecedents are considered. Polk's understanding of the American Union derived from his belief in the radical dogmas of the American Revolution.[1] The Union of the colonies had arisen as a barrier against corrupt consolidations of political and economic power, not as a scheme for dividing up or developing the riches of the New World. The basis for building a unified economic order did not exist, for economic conflicts among the colonies were both real and natural. The glue that might hold the Union together was not the promise of wealth, but fear, fear of arbitrary and unjust grants of privilege and power. Territorial expansion would provide a further diffusion of political and economic power, thus placing the potential for political and economic consolidation beyond the capacities of the general government. Wealth had been widely diffused for over two centuries, and any change in that order of distribution could mean only one thing, that the many would be taxed for the benefit of the few. Jefferson had bought Louisiana as a hedge against such consolidations, and Polk fought his war for the same reasons. The manifest destiny of the nation was not that it should be rich and powerful, but that it should be self-governing. That the constitutional Union of 1789 fell into shambles in less than three generations can be understood only as a lapse of common will to honor and preserve "the same spirit of harmony and compromise in which it was formed."[2]

On May 17, 1847, Henry Hubbard, former U.S. senator from New Hampshire and then U.S. subtreasurer in Boston, wrote Polk congratulating him on "the brilliant successes" that had attended recent military operations in Mexico. He observed that, having just returned from a visit to his native state, he could report that public sentiments there favored the Mexican War. He expressed dismay that in Boston he had become "accustomed to hear very different language from men in and out of office, from men whose hearts were callous to every patriotic feeling and whose lips were constantly giving utterance to their treasonable feelings." The sons of New Hampshire evidenced the proper sentiments, he thought, for "they tell well for the country and give assurance" that the nation's free institutions would not fail, notwithstanding "the violence of Massachusetts treason." Having laid out his estimate of the diverse directions of popular thought in New England, Hubbard urged the president to visit New Hampshire during the summer.[3]

Hubbard's invitation set forth most of the operative considerations that might have influenced Polk's decision to tour New England in the summer of 1847. Military victories at Monterrey and Buena Vista had put to rest Whig charges that inadequate preparation and administrative mismanagement would bring disaster and dishonor to the nation's fighting forces. Public opinion in New England no longer followed Massachusetts' violent antipathies against the war. Conditions for healing the war's divisive effects were now favorable, and the president's presence in that quarter of the nation would aid the process of bringing the people together. Flushed with victory, the chief executive could now extend an olive branch to his highly vocal and discordant opposition.

During the course of his prior twenty years in political service, Polk had seldom waived the flag of American patriotism, manifest or otherwise. On the other hand, he had never joined the ranks of those southerners threatening disunion over abolition petitions, protective tariffs, or any other regional sensitivity. He had taken his political views from his grandfather, Ezekiel Polk, and that political inheritance had placed him squarely in line with the dogmas of the revolutionary and Jeffersonian radicals, whose notion of the Union was much more spiritual than political. Indeed, the dreamers of the early republic had begun with a unity of spirit, not a spirit of union. It was one thing to fight together, another to grow together. Grandpa Polk had fought for the revolutionary promises of political and personal freedom; his several treks westward from the North Carolina frontier to that of west Tennessee demonstrated a colonial mind-set that resisted the strictures of an established, consolidated, and enforced social order.

Independence from Great Britain could not change two centuries of colonial thought and feeling respecting the virtues of salutary neglect. Polk was a grandson of both the revolution and the frontier. As president of the Dialectic Society at the University of North Carolina, the country's future president had attended collegiate debates on the expediency of westward expansion. Thirty years later he would go to New England to make peace with those yet opposed to the traditions of a frontier union. On that tour President Polk would take great pains to avoid making public mention of his governmental and military policies. He did not wish to debate divisive issues with his opponents. He would let the handshaking do the talking, both to the American people and to their foreign adversaries. Besides, continued divisions at home might render peace negotiations with Mexico all the more difficult. Polk would not allow the Mexicans to win in Washington what they could not win on the battlefield. So he would keep his counsel and seek reconciliation with those whose further opposition to the war would continue only for want of an occasion to save face.[4]

Anticipating that during his forthcoming tour of the Northeast he would have neither time nor energy to keep his diary current, President Polk skipped forty pages between his entries for June 22 and July 7, 1847. Clearly the president intended to make retrospective entries for the intervening fifteen days of intensive travel and speech making. In the event, Polk turned to John Appleton, chief clerk of the Navy Department, to write a journal of the northern tour; and upon receipt of Appleton's rather lengthy account, Polk found that he had left too few pages blank. He briefly noted where he had traveled on each of the fifteen days and retained Appleton's bound manuscript as an addendum to his presidential diary.

Following the death of the president in 1849, John Appleton's journal remained in the custody of Mrs. Polk until her death in 1891. In 1897 Mrs. Polk's niece and heir, Mrs. George W. Fall, gave Appleton's journal to Judge Jacob McGavock Dickinson, in whose family's possession the bound manuscript remained until 1926. On October 22, 1926, Jacob McGavock Dickinson, Jr., gave the journal to the Polk Memorial

President James K. Polk. (*Courtesy Texas Humanities Resource Center*)

Association of Nashville to be kept with other Polk memorabilia. Now for the first time John Appleton's journal has been proposed for publication, some one hundred thirty-seven years after its composition. Generations of historians have had but scanty knowledge of the existence of this rare and illuminating account of President Polk's wartime travels.

In Appleton's journal, scholars will find the record of an insider's view of the president's tumultuous receptions in Baltimore, Philadelphia, New York, Boston, Concord, and Augusta. It would be difficult to overstate the historical value of Appleton's largely unknown eyewitness record of the public's response to President Polk and, in turn, to his conduct of the war with Mexico. Historians unfriendly to "Mr. Polk's War" generally have played down the popularity of his presidency in the northern states, leaving his place in history rather more negative than that allowed by his contemporaries. John Appleton's journal provides a partial corrective to the notion that northerners generally opposed both the Mexican War and the president under whose personal direction the conflict was expanded and fought.

Appleton's journal claims another point of uniqueness. Seldom in one historical record do national and local history blend together so completely. Local responses to Polk's tour had indirect national consequences; on the other hand, Polk's tour revealed much of what local leaders thought was consequential for the president to see and experience in their community. For example, New Yorkers thought that their local water aqueduct was truly one of the wonders of their great city. Boston's Whig leaders proudly pointed to their free public schools as "the peculiar institution of the North." Thus the reader of the journal "sees" the northeastern urban centers as Polk and local leaders saw the state of their civilization, including its architecture, humanitarian institutions, industrial progress, commercial growth, and, perhaps most importantly, its people.

President Polk's correspondence provides a different though related perspective from which to examine this very important trip northward. Many of the letters, of course, convey official invitations and presidential responses; others detail partisan infighting between local Democrats and Whigs with respect to Polk's visit. Viewed collectively and in tandem with Appleton's journal, the letters show the reader at first hand the divisive effects of the nation's war with Mexico and Polk's personal efforts to contain the growth of antiwar sentiment in the Northeast, much of which had been nurtured and fed by opposition newspapers in the early months of the war.

No negative aspect of the war's management in Washington escaped the attention of the Whig press in America. Conversely, Democratic newspapers knew no bounds in their praise of the president's expansionist policies. It would be but a slight exaggeration to say that an unbiased, nonpartisan press barely existed during the second party system, and those newspapers without specific party backing often took decided stands on the war issue, thus slanting their news coverage as suited their owner's point of view. The party presses devoted their columns almost entirely to political affairs and to commercial concerns. The more independent or "sensationalist" sheets extended their coverage to those remarkable and timely events that commanded two-cent's worth of curiosity from the reader on the street. The two-penny presses lived on the excitements of the day, not the annual subscriptions of the party faithful. Although the popular presses may have overdramatized their news stories, their attention almost always certified the reality of like public tastes and interests. As witnesses go, reporters in Polk's day were predictable in their biases; and to that extent they may be usable if not always reliable.

From these three types of evidence—diaries, letters, and newspapers—it is possible to retrace the president's progress eastward and analyze its internal dynamics. This kind of testimony will not quantify what may have been the political consequences of his trip. However interesting such calculations might be, their use would probably prove misleading, for neither the president nor his opponents expected the electorate's political persuasions to be greatly changed by the demonstration of presidential power or the charisma of its standard-bearer. Electioneering in the second party system seldom turned many voters away from the principles of their fathers. No, the function of the political rally was to arouse the voting corps to unity and action. For most voters, the decisive choice came on the question of whether or not to vote. Viewed in that special sense of the word *political*, Polk could say quite truthfully that he planned to make a "nonpolitical" excursion, for most of the eastern congressional elections had already been held.[5]

The president and his wife left Washington on Tuesday, June 22, accompanied by Attorney General Nathan Clifford, Patent Commissioner Edmund Burke, and Chief Clerk John Appleton of the Navy

Department. All the members of Polk's cabinet, his private secretary, J. Knox Walker, and a large number of friends, attended his leave-taking, which involved no formal ceremony. The noon train departed fifteen minutes late. Sarah Childress Polk and her niece, Johanna Rucker, traveled with the president only as far as Baltimore, where they would stay the night and then head westward for a month's visit with their family in Tennessee. Appleton observed in his journal that as rapid as their progress was by locomotive, their conveyance was but a "slow coach" when compared with the signals passing at lightning speed over the telegraph wires such as kept them company along the way. The cars traveled forty miles to the outskirts of Baltimore in one hour and forty minutes, having reached on occasion "exhilarating" speeds of nearly forty miles per hour.[6]

Indeed, the only major difficulty in making arrangements for the president's visit to Baltimore had arisen over prospects that the official party might arrive too early in the day to suit the convenience of the city's Whig mayor, Jacob G. Davies. The mayor had worried that if the president took the ten o'clock cars and arrived earlier than expected, appropriate parade and ceremony for his entrance into the city might become disordered. Louis McLane, former head of the Treasury and secretary of state under Andrew Jackson, had advised Polk the day before to take the noon cars and had assured him that he might "regulate the speed and stopping of the train" as would suit his own pleasure. As president of the Baltimore and Ohio Railway Company, McLane took pride in assigning to Polk a special car for his journey. It would be the first use made of the luxurious vehicle, which reportedly cost $2,000 to construct. Municipal pride required that all arrangements for the visit be correct in every regard, particularly since the official hosts were members of the opposition political party.[7]

At the outer depot Polk was warmly greeted by "a multitude of those hardy sons of toil" who worked in Baltimore's dingy industrial precincts, noted for their smoky forges, engines, and workshops. It had been a difficult week for the citizens of Baltimore, besieged as they were by one of the worst periods of sickness in their history. Some eighty-four deaths the previous week had been visited upon their populace, striking most heavily among children under the age of two years. But the sovereigns rose to the occasion of a presidential visit and lined the avenues of their business district to see the chief magistrate pass in an open barouche pulled by four white horses. Twenty companies of troops, accompanied by their respective bands of music, stood at attention along the parade route. Spectators waving banners filled the upper windows, and thousands of people crowded into the streets below. The procession came to rest at the Exchange Hotel, into which the president was conducted with haste, just in time to avoid a drenching shower. Mayor Davies took the presidential party into a private apartment and gave a brief address of welcome, to which the president responded with equal brevity. He then went to the hotel lobby and for over three hours held an open reception for all comers, including such groups as the Association of the Defenders of Baltimore, the Junior Artillery, and the student body of the Eastern Female High School. A sumptuous dinner with vintage wines interrupted the handshaking at six-thirty, but at eight the president resumed his place in the lobby and for two hours more greeted citizens waiting their moment of introduction. Mrs. Polk, who upon arrival had been driven to the Exchange Hotel in a closed carriage and who had not been included in the parade, ceremonies, or dinner, held her own reception for the ladies of those gentlemen engaged in official duties downstairs. At midnight the Independent Blues almost closed the day with a brief serenade of band music; however, at one o'clock fire broke out nearby, and nearly every church bell in the city responded with a noisy and steady peal.[8]

Rising for an early breakfast at six and bidding leave of Mrs. Polk and her party, the president and his aides took an express train of cars departing for Wilmington at seven-ten "at a most gratifying momentum." Stops at Havre de Grace, Cecil, and Elkton slowed their progress. At each little village the president went to the rear of his car and greeted those who had gathered to see him pass. At ten o'clock the train arrived in Wilmington, and city authorities invited the presidential party to use the town hall for an informal welcome by the venerable veteran of the Revolutionary War and former congressman, Samuel B. Davis. Polk complimented the industry and energy of the city's people, noting that their great prosperity was more likely the result of their local labors than of those policies adopted in Washington City. Here the president articulated one of his most frequent themes, a line that projected rhetorical modesty on his part and general satisfaction with his success. it was a discreet way of saying to the public, in the presence of the Whig leadership, "My opponents claimed that my tariff and war policies would bring financial ruin and military destruction to your community, but I thank you for proving them wrong!" The crowds loved his polite barbs and took his veiled boasts with good humor and marked approval. Thus the president played his part with conspicuous ease, never failing to notice the many evidences of prosperity at every hand.[9]

Fortunately for Polk's press coverage in Baltimore and Wilmington, one of the Washington correspondents of the two-penny *New York Herald* had joined the presidential party in Baltimore. Other reporters from Philadelphia, New York City, and Boston subsequently traveled with the president's entourage, and Appleton recorded their names in his journal. He did not do so for the *Herald's* letter writer. Appleton made a point of noting in his journal that "*The Doctor,* of the Herald, had now joined us, also, and faithfully reported the President's progress and receptions throughout our entire journey." Publishing only under his pen name, "The Doctor" wrote his story with such color and detail that newspapers all over the country carried his accounts. Except for the president, no one in the traveling party contributed more to the trip's success story than the *Herald's* mystery reporter. His sympathetic and knowing letters on the Texas question, Americans in California, Mexican War reports, and inside views of Polk's administration might have earned him a minor place in the history of his times had he not hid behind his pseudonym.[10]

Following a refreshing collation at the conclusion of the public ceremonies in Wilmington, the presidential procession regrouped and drove to the docks where the steamer *George Washington* waited for the trip upriver to Philadelphia. Officials in the Custom House in Philadelphia had wanted the president to arrive by train, but Democratic friends there had opposed the notion of bringing him in from Wilmington through the dust. At a public meeting they had persuaded Mayor John Swift, a Whig, to arrange for the presidential party to arrive by steamer, thus permitting the Navy Yard to give the proper salute and allowing more citizens the opportunity of observing the president's arrival. The steamer *George Washington* had come to Wilmington that morning laden with dignitaries from the Quaker City and prepared for luncheon festivities to be observed on the return trip. Shortly before noon the *George Washington* got under way and steamed past numerous friendly demonstrations en route to Philadelphia. The vessel passed the Navy Yard at ten minutes past two and proceeded up river as far as the Dyottville glass works, turned about, and came to at the Navy Yard an hour later. Appleton recorded the president's arrival in the following fashion:

> The wharves all along the City's front, and the shipping (all of which had flags flying to the breeze) were crowded with people, who cheered enthusiastically, as our gallant steamer pursued her way. Meanwhile our friends in Jersey as well as in Philadelphia made the welkin ring with oft-repeated thunder from their well-managed ordnance; and heavy reports, also, from the Cutter Forward, just above the Navy Yard, gave life and animation to the scene.
>
> At ten minutes past three o'clock, the President and Suite, and the Philadelphia Committee of Arrangements, landed at the Navy Yard Wharf, under a national salute, and met with a glorious reception. The Yard itself, the tops of houses, the streets, lanes and alleys, in the vicinity of the landing, were crowded with thousands of eager spectators, all intent upon seeing and honoring the distinguished head of their Country.

At four-thirty a procession, headed by a military escort "consisting of a troop of cavalry, a regiment of artillery, and a regiment of infantry, with bands of music at appropriate intervals," began its three-hour march into the city. Polk's barouche and twenty-seven other carriages were followed by a rear guard of military units that included three troops of cavalry and three brigades each of artillery and infantry. Over forty thousand people viewed the street parade, which ended at Vice-President George B. Dallas's residence in Walnut Street. A large crowd of five thousand filled the street in front of Dallas's home and repeatedly called for the president to come out and address them. The vice-president finally appeared and urged the mob of well-wishers to greet their distinguished guest at Independence Hall on the next afternoon. Fatigue had finally caught up with the president, and thus he excused himself from all further public duties that evening, except for auditing a midnight serenade by the combined efforts of the Breiter Association, the Maennerchor, and the Leidertofel Society, whose instrumental and vocal performances delighted the thousands of people keeping watch in Walnut Street.[11]

The next morning the president toured Philadelphia with Vice-President Dallas and members of the host committee. They first inspected Girard College, the central building of which was thought to be among the most impressive in the young republic. From there the party went to the Eastern Penitentiary and visited some of its inmates in their cells. City fathers had intended a tour of the Fairmount Water Works, but according to Appleton, "the President had been increasingly threatened with illness, since he left Baltimore, and he felt obliged now to husband his strength." So the president returned to his quarters and rested for two hours before going to the Chester Street preparatory or "Model School," which was divided into three departments, a grammar school for young boys, one for young girls, and a co-educational secondary school for higher studies. Patriotic songs from the children, brief speeches of welcome, and a visit to each department highlighted the president's visit. He next toured the Central High School for boys, which then numbered some four hundred students. His visit there was quite brief, as he had fallen behind schedule and was yet obliged to tour the Philadelphia Mint. At the mint he viewed the entire process of making coins and took particular interest in observing the workmen strike a medal bearing his image and the date of his election. From the mint he went to the Old State House in Independence Square, where large crowds had gathered for the mayor's and councils' official welcome. After two hours of handshaking, the president returned at three o'clock to the Dallas residence for a brief rest. [12]

At five o'clock the president rose for an elegant dinner party given by the vice-president. Then at seven the president was "hurried off" to the Northern Liberties Hall, Philadelphia's version of Tammany Hall, for a political rally. A couple of hours of speaking and greeting, said by Appleton to have been "rather too exciting to be pleasant," would have exhausted any healthy person; yet Polk gathered himself together and attended a late-evening military ball hosted by Maj. Gen. Robert Patterson. It was said to have been a "princely" levee, one that filled the general's magnificent mansion with elegant "female beauty and military display striving for preeminence." The president excused himself from "this brilliant scene" early and returned to his quarters. Yet another midnight serenade lengthened yet another long day. [13]

On the following morning the president crossed the Delaware River into Camden, where he was greeted by an artillery salute and a large crowd of citizens. Commodore Charles Stewart, much celebrated in the War of 1812 and upwards of seventy years old, had now joined the president's official party and attracted considerable interest among northerners, who had had little prior opportunity to see or meet "Old

Ironsides." For the first time in any public speeches, Polk's friends mentioned the Mexican War. Welcoming the president to Camden, Capt. John W. Mickle brought the war and Polk's tour into focus.

> Mr President, I am happy in the opportunity of welcoming you to the State of New Jersey. We bid you welcome, not only as President of the United States, but individually we bid you welcome. We trust, Sir, that the prosperity of the country, never greater than at present, may continue, and that the war which has been forced upon us by the enemy, may be ended as it has begun, in a blaze of glory. Again, Sir, we welcome you to our State.

Polk replied that he rejoiced to hear of the prosperous condition of the citizens of New Jersey and expressed his regret that he could not extend his visit. His special train of cars, "gaily decorated with flags," proceeded then toward South Amboy, stopping along the way for welcoming demonstrations at Bordentown, Burlington, and Hightsville. Arriving at South Amboy ahead of schedule, the presidential party waited for the arrival of the steamer *Cornelius Vanderbilt* from New York City.[14]

The steamer *Eureka* brought the first wave of New Yorkers, including sundry committees of arrangements and a brass band. Shortly after their arrival, the steamer *Vanderbilt* landed, and the president boarded one of the nation's most luxurious vessels for his entry into the nation's richest and most populous city. Commodore Vanderbilt personally served as captain and pilot of his vessel. Its deck was filled with dignitaries, who strained to hear Alderman Morris Franklin greet their distinguished visitor in behalf of New York City's Board of Aldermen and its Common Council. He gracefully spoke of his fellow citizens' wish to put aside partisan spirit in favor of "the overflowings of patriotic and grateful hearts for the liberal dispensations of an overruling and bountiful Providence." He depicted the spirit of his city as being one that warmly supported humanitarian institutions. "We can present to you institutions, fostered and encouraged by the protecting care of a philanthropic Government, where poverty and disease receive protection and relief, where the deaf and the dumb, the orphan and the blind, without regard to age, nativity or color, are the objects of our sympathy and regard." The alderman pointed further to his city's achievements in religion, science, literature, and commerce. He allowed that while many might think "that Mammon is the God of our idolatry," yet he

would bravely add that "the crowning monument of our City's enterprise, is that noble aqueduct which, from a source of fifty miles dis-
tributes within our midst the pure exhilarating contents of the Croton
Lake, affording protection in time of danger, and a delightful beverage
to all." Considering the dangers of bad water and sickness in Baltimore, the weary president must have heard this latter boast with no
little relief.[15]

Polk responded to the alderman's welcome with sentiments of high
regard for New York City's great wealth, enterprise, and benevolent institutions. He then suggested in his quiet way the idea that wealth and
freedom have their price.

> In the City of New York, we have a representation of the whole republic,
> and from its prosperity some idea may be formed of the power and re-
> sources of the nation. The extent of those resources can as yet only be
> imagined; but if our countrymen are true to their free institutions and to
> their invaluable Union, there is nothing in the future of grandeur and of
> glory, which we may not anticipate for our beloved country. Already we
> have increased, within little more than half a century, from four millions
> to twenty millions, but he who shall live to see the President of the
> United States, fifty years hence, will welcome the representative of a
> hundred millions of people.

The president made it through his remarks and then went below to one
of the cabins to lie down. Appleton thought it "surprising how, under
such circumstances, he was enabled to sustain himself so well." Polk
had come north into the hotbeds of antiwar dissent because he thought
his country's freedom and Union required it, and he would neither stop
nor turn back for want of easy health.[16]

No expense was considered in bidding the president welcome, for
national pride and local boosterism dictated that a city of so many recently and fully washed rich should not be "outdone" by the older and
more established aristocracies of Philadelphia and Boston. The entire
assembly of five hundred guests on board the *Vanderbilt* then moved
downstairs to the grand salon and sat down to tables that were "literally
loaded with every thing which could delight the palate, and the richest wines were provided in unmeasured abundance." As the steamer
passed Perth Amboy, the *Eureka* passed ahead of the *Vanderbilt* and
fired its salute. Then the steamer *Zephyr*, swarming with passengers,
exchanged salutes. The Coney Island boat *American Eagle* next ap-
proached and gave its mark of honor. Before passing Fort Hamilton,

the president returned to the deck and received the reports of that installation's heavy guns. The ordnance depot at Governor's Island joined the firing of cannons from numerous revenue cutters, foreign ships of war, and merchant vessels. Hundreds of ships jockeyed for positions close to the *Vanderbilt* as the president's steamer landed at Castle Garden, where a crowd of over ten thousand awaited their guest's arrival.

There Mayor William Brady bid the president officially welcome, and Polk struggled to offer a few lines in reply. Press accounts described him as looking "worn and fatigued," his grey hair hanging close and his face wet with perspiration. The band played "Hail to the Chief," and amid choruses of cheers and applause, the mayor took the president to an elegant barouche drawn by four matched greys. The procession into the city included fifty carriages escorted by a large corps of cavalry. The Society of Tammany followed the carriages and marched with its own bands and two companies of light guards. Companies from the fire department and deputations from the several wards made up another division of the parade. Then countless brigades of artillery, companies of militiamen, and bands of music brought up the rear guard. The line of march moved down Broadway to Astor Place, through Astor Place to the Bowery, down the Bowery to Chatham Street, and down Chatham to the City Hall, from which place the president reviewed the trailing units of the parade. Crowds in excess of 140,000 cheered the two-mile-long procession, which took over an hour to pass. The heat of the day was as intense as the people's welcome was warm. As Appleton observed with considerable understatement, "There is no place for a crowd like New York."[17]

The next day's schedule began with an early-morning walk with the mayor through the Fulton and Washington markets. Despite efforts to avoid public notice, the president was recognized by some of the grocers and their customers. At ten o'clock the President went to City Hall and greeted the public, which according to Appleton included "lawyers, physicians, and divines, *Litterateurs*, merchants, officeholders, and clerks, loafers, and brokers." It was a dense multitude and included even some females. Two regiments of volunteers for the Mexican War came through the receiving line, as did numerous foreign consuls residing in New York City. At noon the presidential party made a "flying visit" to Brooklyn, which repeated the previous day's scenes of huge crowds, tumultuous shouts, military display, and cannons roaring. At two-thirty the Brooklyn Committee returned the president to the care of his hosts in the city, and the official party now headed for the High Bridge.[18]

On the way there were stops at the Forty-second Street Distributing Reservoir, a deaf and dumb asylum, Nowlan's Restaurant, an orphan house, and McComb's Dam. At six-thirty the entourage of eleven carriages reached the High Bridge, which when completed would convey water from Croton Lake to the half a million people of New York City. An imposing structure, it was easily the most ambitious undertaking yet devised in the New World. The next stop was at the new York Asylum for the blind on Ninth Street, where a large number of spectators gathered with the students to share the festivities. The president expressed pleasure at having the opportunity to return the visit paid him in 1846 by a group of students from the asylum, including Miss Fanny Crosby, who rose and recited a poem she had written for the occasion of Polk's visit. Pressed for time, the presidential party left without taking supper and returned to the Astor House. There a committee from Tammany Hall greeted the president and escorted him across the park to their Wigwam. With appropriate and highly secret ceremonials, the New York Democracy initiated their president into the Tammany Society. Quite exhausted by his hectic schedule, Polk made a very short speech to the largest and most devoted group of Democrats with whom he would meet during his travels. "I appear before you this evening so much fatigued with the exertions which I have made, that I feel wholly unable to address you as I could wish." Thus he passed up his best opportunity to try to compose the growing rifts in New York's Democracy, divisions largely occasioned by ex-President Martin Van Buren's opposition to the war. Van Buren's absence drew no public notice from the president, but he resented the distance and division that it represented. Perhaps the president could not say anything of serious matters for both political as well as physical reasons. As he retired to the Astor House, a serenade from another German band closed his Saturday night in New York.[19]

On Sunday, Polk welcomed a day of rest and went to church three times. In the morning he went to St. Bartholomew's Episcopal Church with Mayor Brady. At that service the president heard a sermon preached on the text, "For the wages of sin is death; but the gift of God is eternal life." In the afternoon Benjamin F. Butler escorted the president to a Presbyterian service. The preacher seized the occasion to ask whether the religion of Christ and patriotism were compatible. He held that they were, that it was important for Christians to pray for their nation's leaders, that ministers of the gospel should speak out on public issues, that the use of martial arms in service to one's country was not contrary to Christ's teachings, and that "the community should not be led away by the mere fanatical designs of political enthusiasts" on the question of slavery, for that institution "would eventually give way before enlightenment." All of this and more on Catholic immigration and temperance came to his lips straight from Psalm 137. Sunday evening the president, accompanied by Alderman James D. Oliver, attended the Dutch Reformed Church at the corner of Fourth Street and Lafayette place. The preacher chose for his text the fourth verse of St. Mark's ninth chapter: "And there appeared unto them, Elisha with Moses; and they were talking with Jesus." Thus three members of New York's reverend clergy had preached to the president on such diverse topics as the wages of sin, Christian patriotism, and the transfiguration. It was good day's piety for any politician, even for one who regularly attended services on Sundays.[20]

Early the next morning the president and his party boarded the steamer *Hero* for New Haven, where they were expected at midmorning. The *New Haven Herald* had anticipated Polk's arrival by extending a public invitation to all who might wish to join in the procession from the landing to the City Hall and by recalling Polk's private visit to New Haven in November of 1834. On that occasion the youthful congressman from Tennessee had brought his brother Samuel W. Polk, his nephews James and Knox Walker, and William T. Cooper (son of a friend) to New Haven for their matriculation into Yale College. Polk personally had selected and furnished the boys' rooms and had remained several days attending to their affairs. In this very indirect way the *New Haven Herald* claimed the president as a longtime friend, whose welcome should be warm and generous.[21]

Secretary of State James Buchanan, accompanied by Captain Enoch Steen—recently furloughed hero of the Battle of Buena Vista— now traveled with the president and brought him an update on affairs in Washington City. The *Hero* landed at New Haven about eleven o'clock, and after an hour's procession into the city and through its major streets, the long line of carriages and military units stopped at the public square in front of City Hall. Although there were no formal speeches, the president did receive as many who came through the reception line. Then it was off to the campus of Yale College, where the president visited the College Chapel and heard the chorus of the Yale Beethoven Society sing the national hymn, "My Country 'Tis of Thee," to the tune of "God Save the Queen." Then the president inspected the John Trumbull Gallery and the college library. A large and vocal group of Yale students cheered the president as he left the campus and crossed the street to the Tontine House for lunch. His schedule did not include a thirty-minute wait for the meal, and with due apologies he completed only the soup course and left for the railroad depot to take the cars to Hartford.[22]

The heat of the day, estimated at 90 degrees in early afternoon, forced open the windows of the cars, and the entire ensemble of dignitaries, some thirty in number, breathed dust and smoke all the way to Hartford. The enormous crowd of thirty thousand at Hartford came as something of a pleasant surprise, for the city's entire population was something below twenty thousand. For two hours the president's cavalcade inched its way through the congested streets. "The Doctor" reported to the *New York Herald* that because of the blistering sun, it was "the most dreadful ordeal we have ever experienced." After refreshments at the City Hotel, the party took the cars on to Springfield, their final stop of the day. Again the ringing of church bells, the firing of guns, and the searching looks of friendly faces welcomed the president, who was delighted by the late-night reception and elegant supper prepared at Warrener's Hotel.[23]

After breakfasting at seven, the president and his aids boarded a special train for Boston, some ninety miles and four hours away. It was a cloudy morning, and as the train paused at the Worcester depot for the president to greet the public, heavy rains began to fall and continued throughout the day. Reaching Boston precisely at noon, the president received the greetings of Mayor Josiah Quincy and the city's Board of Aldermen and Common Council. In the course of his brief remarks, the mayor urged the president to an examination of New England's institutions, "particularly of the free school, the peculiar institution of our land, by which, with the blessing of Heaven, we hope to continue a race of intelligent freemen, who will understand, maintain and transmit the liberties and virtues of their fathers to the end of time." In his equally brief remarks the president rejoined that with regard to public education he would be pleased "to witness the prosperity which has crowned your efforts, in whatever has for its object the improvement of the people or the honor of our common country." The entrance parade lasted two hours, and but for the drenching rains Boston's welcome might have been as spectacular as that of New York City's.[24]

Appleton observed in his journal that the people of Boston were not accountable for the weather, "any more than they were for the article in the Boston Advertiser, advising them not to receive the President with public honors." It had also rained in Boston on a summer day in 1843, when President John Tyler paid his presidential respects. Upon Polk's arrival at the Revere House, Massachusetts's governor, George N. Briggs, officially welcomed him to the Commonwealth and expressed the wishes of his people that they might ever and faithfully fulfill their obligations to the Union. Polk took up the governor's reference to the Union and observed that "however much we may differ about local or temporary questions of policy, on the question of Union, we are all united." After two hours of handshaking, the president rested briefly before preparing for dinner.[25]

If the rains had dampened the enthusiasm of the afternoon, the banquet that evening brought cold anger to members of the official party. A hundred and fifty guests filled the Revere House dining room, and an extravagant bill of fare filled the tables as a fine band of musicians played in the background. According to Appleton's account, "The temperance question had been recently agitated in the city councils, and the mayor had declined presiding at the tables in the presence of wine. It was determined, therefore, to banish wine, and retain the mayor." Appleton thought the decision a hypocritical one, since the host committee had provided their hotel rooms "with a plentiful supply of liquors." He did not know "which was in worse taste—the frigid temperance of the dining hall, or the bar-room supply of the sleeping chambers." After making a few remarks about the etiquette of the occasion, the mayor dispensed with sentiments and bumpers and escorted the president from the room. "They were followed at once from the hall by nearly all the guests, who seemed to be unanimously of opinion that a cold-water dinner was not entitled to more than an hour and a half's attention." Appleton, a future congressman from Maine, knew

Boston to be a city with a noble history and a generous heart but possessed of an enigmatic ethic.

> It is greedy after wealth, but then it spends it like a prince. It is a little puritan in its notions, but puritanism is better than its reverse, and after all, wine may be had, even in Boston, if it is drunk in secret. It clamors against war, but it supplies good soldiers. It has sometimes given birth to moral treason; but it has always contained a pure leaven of uncorruptible patriotism.

What really wounded Appleton's pride was that the Whig mayor had avoided toasting the president by making "a needless sacrifice to bigotry." For his part, Polk wrote his wife, Sarah, that although he was becoming "much fatigued," he was "much gratified" with his visit to New England thus far and would continue his tour as planned.[26]

The following day Polk saw the usual tourist sights, including Faneuil Hall, Quincy Market, and the Bunker Hill Monument in Charlestown. From Charlestown the presidential party traveled by the cars to Lowell for an inspection of the textile factories, the workers of which had been given the day off. In his remarks the president played to the thousands of laborers who welcomed him at the depot.

> The history of our country is closely identified with its workingmen, its self-taught and self-made men. They are the secret of its strength, its rapid progress, and of the foundation of our free institutions. They are the true bone and sinew of the country, and not only of our country but of the world. They are our true sovereigns. You, sir, are my sovereign, and I am but your servant.

At his lodgings, the Merrimack House, ten thousand spectators awaited his arrival. After a brief rest, the city fathers gave Polk a luncheon at Mechanics Hall for two hundred guests. Afterward Polk held an open reception, and later in the afternoon he toured the great waterworks that powered the factories. Among the more memorable scenes of Lowell were the thousands of women mill workers who lined the cavalcade route, the unusual number of flags displayed, and the text of one large banner strung across Centre Street, "Welcome, the Chief Magistrate of the Union: Our Country, however bounded." The presidential party retired early, but not before a local band had played its version of the midnight serenade.[27]

On the next morning the president toured the Babel factories with Mayor Jefferson Bancroft, who twenty-five years before had worked as a mill hand in one of the Lowell factories. Appleton observed that they had entered "a carpet, a cotton, a cassimere, a calico, printing, establishment, saw any number of machines, both dumb and human, [and] wondered a little at the extensive and costly scale on which every thing was managed. . . ." He found the experience depressing when he considered that the workers were "shut up twelve hours a day, amid so much noise, in so bad an atmosphere, and with such mechanical employment. . . ." Appleton thought that the true republican spirit could not flourish in any town with such a large dependent population; at heart he was a believer in the agrarian way of life. After breakfast the presidential entourage left Lowell by the cars to spend the day in Concord, which the traveling party reached at mid-morning after brief stops at Nashua and Manchester. Quartered at Gass's American House, the president held an open reception in the upper gallery of the front portico. At two o'clock he went to the State House for a joint meeting of the new Hampshire legislature. The presiding officer of the convention, Moses Norris, Jr., welcomed Polk to New Hampshire and in so doing made veiled references to public support for Polk's war efforts.

> These crowded galleries and hall, the thronged streets and avenues of this usually quiet town, bespeak the ardent wishes of the people to see you, and to exchange congratulations, as American Citizens, with the Chief Executive Magistrate of our great and flourishing Union. This proclaims your welcome more forcibly than any words I can utter. Though in New England, and especially in New Hampshire, we have a climate of frosts and snows for a large part of the year, a country of rugged (though, at this season of the year, of beautiful and charming) aspect, yet we have a population, energetic, bold, and ready at all times to defend the country and its institutions, but of warm hearts and hospitable feelings.

Polk took something of a philosophical bent in his address to the legislators. He called to mind New Hampshire's history and progress in the past seventy years since independence. Then he laid out what was uppermost in his mind.

> To this people is confided the last hope of man for well-regulated self government, and if our system fails, where shall we look hereafter, for another experiment which shall hold out a higher promise of success! . . . To sustain my country's interests and preserve her honor unimpaired, has been, also, my effort in the station I have been called to occupy, at a momentous period of public affairs. In this period, great questions have

arisen and been decided, whose final results, must excite the most earnest interest of the whole union. Whatever they may be, I have the consciousness, to rest on, of having endeavored to faithfully discharge my duty, always humbly relying on the Providence of Him in whose hands are the destinies of men and of nations.

The president's address did not labor his principal theme, for his presence in New England and the citizenry's warm response spoke with more force than any rhetorical power at his disposal. He had come to New England at the suggestion of Henry Hubbard, whose reading of the public mind of New Hampshire had proven to be fully accurate. After the joint session was adjourned, Governor Jared W. Williams hosted a dinner at Gass's Hall, where the food was "enlivened by claret, madeira, sherry, and champagne." The president and his official party returned to the State House at six to receive a large gathering of citizens. Appleton noted that "Mr Buchanan was of course not absent on this occasion, and among the ladies the bachelor premier was almost a match for the married President." At eight-thirty the party retraced their morning's journey and arrived at Lowell two hours later.[28]

The next day Polk and his party took the cars for Portland, Maine, and en route stopped at Wilmington Junction, Haverhill, Exeter, New Market, Dover, and South Berwick. The train arrived at Portland at eleven-thirty, and Governor John W. Dana was waiting at the depot to make the official welcoming speech. Surrounded by "a living ocean of humanity," the president's procession then moved up State Street, which was lined on either side with the pupils of the public schools, all dressed in uniform. After dinner at the U.S. Hotel, the party took the steamer *Huntress* down the bay and then up the Kennebeck River to Hallowell. Although the hour was well past midnight, the citizens of Augusta lighted their windows and those of the State House to celebrate the president's arrival. Thousands of citizens followed the cavalcade through the city to the sounds of booming cannons and ringing church bells. it was at the least a happy and "splendid spectacle." Former Senator Reuel Williams opened his large home to the president, and the other members of the party stayed at other private residences in the town.[29]

On Saturday the president spoke to a joint meeting of the Maine legislature. He chose for his theme the nation's "legacy of freedom." He noted that since the founding of the present Union, some fifty-eight years before, the population of the country had multiplied by a factor of seven, and her borders now included the Gulf of Mexico and the Pacific Ocean. The freedom of her people was "the surest safeguard of human liberty throughout the world." He held that disunion would lead the several states to waste their resources and their energies fighting among themselves. "Destroy the Union, and the last example of freedom to the oppressed will at once be destroyed, and the only hope of man for well-regulated self-government will be lost forever from the earth." He counted it his sacred duty to preserve the Union and rejected the supposed worth of "our little local jealousies and all our divisions of individual opinion." He expressed gratitude that he had been given the privilege of being the first incumbent president to visit the State of Maine, a visit he hoped would cultivate "that feeling of brotherhood and mutual regard, between the North and the South, the East and the West, without which we may not anticipate the perpetuity of our free institutions." He quoted his political mentor, Andrew Jackson, in declaring again, "Our Federal Union—it must be preserved."

The president then expanded the range of his remarks and noted that the steam engine had brought the United States in closer proximity to Europe. He thought that the peoples of that continent were beginning "to feel the influence of our system, and to receive from us liberal and enlightened views. Animated by our example and the successful working of our government, the suffering and oppressed people of the old world begin to understand now their own rights, and to claim the enjoyment, as we enjoy them, of freedom of thought, freedom of speech and freedom of conscience." Recent famines in Europe had led Americans to ship food to those starving masses and in so doing to send them also "the glad tidings of our freedom, prosperity, and glory." He reminded his hearers that their nation was a nation of immigrants and that they held open the doors to "the only free asylum for the oppressed which can be found on earth."

He explained that he had spoken at some length because he felt that he could do no greater service to his country than to express his strong conviction "that the preservation of the Union of these States, is paramount to every other political consideration, and that the same spirit of harmony and compromise in which it was formed, is vitally necessary to secure its existence and perpetuate its blessings." Throughout his journey, the northern limits of which he had now reached, he had witnessed proofs at every hand of the Union's great value and people's attachment to it. He would return to Washington City "with an increased sense of their responsibility and importance, and with a confirmed regard for that venerated Constitution, which I have been sworn faithfully to administer." The spirit of liberty's empire was as much alive in Maine as it was in Washington City or anywhere else where freemen might reside, and the president had traveled to Augusta to make his point in deed as in word.[30]

At the dinner that evening there was but one toast, "the health of the President." Afterward he bid farewell to the people of Augusta and took a carriage for Gardiner, where he would embark for Portland. Throughout his return trip to Washington City he encountered friendly crowds and generous confirmation that his trip north for Union had met with his every anticipation of success.

Conclusion.

Of course, his opposition took a less expansive view of his travels. The *New York Tribune* grudgingly allowed that "we are glad to learn that the President returns in good health, and we shall be much gratified also if he return better qualified to discharge the duties of his office." The Philadelphia *Pennsylvanian* parried the *Tribune's* sarcasm with its own estimate of the president's tour.

> If to see that the popular heart beats high for the Union—if to know that the masses approve the war—if to witness unequalled proofs of prosperity and happiness in every State through which he passed—if these practical evidences of a sound public opinion and a healthy public condition, are calculated to qualify the President better to discharge his duties . . . , there can be no doubt that this Federal newspaper will be gratified.

The editor of the Philadelphia *Pennsylvanian* appreciated the use to which the presidential trip could be put and made a telling argument of it the day following Polk's return to Washington City. The editorialist claimed that the tour's success would certainly "operate most powerfully and heathfully upon public opinion abroad, as well as at home." The Mexican government must conclude that political divisions in the United States over the expediency and conduct of the war did not extend down to the rank-and-file voters, even those of New England.

He thought it supposing too much to conclude that the president's triumphant progress from Baltimore to Augusta "was elicited simply out of respect for the office of Chief Executive of the Nation." Indeed, one must conclude that in time of war such a massive outpouring of public acclaim was in fact an evidence of popular support for the war itself. To formulate a contrary construction of the public's response would require a more tortured pleading than either the evidence or good sense would allow. Late military successes had undercut the popular base for continued Whig opposition, and Polk's tour gave the "loyal opposition" in the Northeast an opportunity to step back from an untenable public position.[31]

NOTES

1. A list of the more useful books on republican ideology in the early national period might include the following works: Bernard Bailyn, *The Ideological Origins of the American Revolution* (Cambridge, Mass: Harvard University Press, 1967) and *The Origins of American Politics* (New York: Knopf, 1968); Lance Banning, *The Jeffersonian Persuasion: Evolution of a Party Ideology* (Ithaca, N.Y.: Cornell University Press, 1978); Richard Buel, Jr., *Securing the Revolution: Ideology in American Politics, 1789–1815* (Ithaca, N.Y.: Cornell University Press, 1972); and Gordon S. Wood, *The Creation of the American Republic, 1776–1787* (Chapel Hill, N.C.: University of North Carolina Press, 1969). In the periodical literature see the following two works: Richard Buel, Jr., "Democracy and the American Revolution: A Frame of Reference," *William and Mary Quarterly* 21 (1964): 165–90; and Robert E. Shalhope, "Toward a Republican Synthesis: The Emergence of an Understanding of Republicanism in American Historiography," *William and Mary Quarterly* 29 (1972): 49–80. For the most thorough consideration to date of the revolutionary ideology, as brought forward into the Jacksonian period, see Robert V. Remini, *Andrew Jackson and the Course of American Freedom, 1822–1832* (New York: Harper & Row, 1981).

2. Quotation from Polk's address to the Maine legislature, July 3, 1847, as reported in the *New York Herald*, July 3, 1847.

3. Henry Hubbard to Polk, May 17, 1847, Papers of James K. Polk, Manuscript Division, Library of Congress, Washington D.C. (hereinafter cited as JKP).

4. Only in the last public address of his journey did he articulate the unspoken purposes of his presence in New England. He began by paying tribute to the spirit of compromise and concession that had supported the formation of the Union, for he marveled at the success with which the founding fathers had brought together under one constitution free people of such "varied pursuits, differing habits and dissimilar institutions." He warned that dissolution of the Union would bring ruin upon the several states and lead their people to waste their resources and efforts warring among themselves. Yet the consequences of the Union's failure would be felt worldwide, for America's experiment in self-government gave hope to oppressed people everywhere. At the close of his address Polk explained that he had spoken at length on the subject of union because he could

do no greater service for his country than to express his deep conviction that "the preservation of the Union of these States, is paramount to every other political consideration. . . ." Polk's address to the Maine legislature, July 3, 1847, as reported in the *New York Herald*, July 3, 1847.

5. Of the eastern seaboard states, only Maryland had not held its regular congressional elections. Some eighteen out of twenty-nine states had held congressional elections prior to June, 1847; of the 161 House members chosen to date, 87 were Whigs, 71 were Democrats, and 3 were independents. The Whigs had gained thirty-two seats and thus expected to control the lower house; the U.S. Senate would remain solidly Democratic in the next Congress. The Democratic reverses in the early congressional elections had preceded, for the most part, U.S. military successes in Mexico.

6. John Appleton, "Journal of a Tour to New England Made by the President in June and July 1847," Polk Memorial Association Collections, Polk Ancestral Home, Columbia, Tenn.; hereafter cited as Appleton's Journal with date of daily entry. The most detailed press account of Polk's visit to Baltimore is in the *New York Herald*, June 25, 1847.

7. Polk to Louis McLane, June 20, 1847, and McLane to Polk, June 21, 1847, JKP; *Niles' Register*, July 3, 1847.

8. Appleton's Journal, June 22, 1847; *New York Herald*, June 23, 24, 25, 1847. Press reports of the 1847 epidemic in Baltimore did not identify the deadly disease or give the total number of fatalities; however, Baltimore's mortality rate jumped by 542, or 16.6 percent. *Niles' Register*, Feb. 5, 1848.

9. Appleton's Journal, June 23, 1847; *New York Herald*, June 25, 1847.

10. Quotation from Appleton's Journal, June 23, 1847. Coincidences of time and place have identified "The Doctor." He had mentioned in one of his 1846 letters to the *Herald* that he stayed in the Astor House in New York City on the evening of Aug. 15, 1846; he took a room there again during President Polk's visit of June 25–27, 1847. George B. Wallis of Washington City registered his name at the Astor on both occasions. Wallis subsequently signed "Dr. G. B. Wallis" under his reminiscence of Lincoln's first inauguration; the publisher of that article identified Wallis as having been "A Contemporary newspaper Correspondent at the Capital." For transcriptions of the Astor House Registers, see *New York Herald*, Aug. 16, 1846, and June 27, 1847. For a reprint of Wallis's article on the Lincoln inauguration and his recollection of Polk's inaugural ball, see "Honest Abe and the Little Giant: A Reminiscence of Lincoln's First Inauguration," *Outlook*, Feb. 9, 1921. According to the *Boston Post* of July 8, 1847, "Dr. Wallace, correspondent of the New York Herald, accompanied the party, as a permanent member of the unofficial suite. . . ."

11. Joel B. Sutherland to Polk, June 17 and 18, 1847, JKP; Daniel T. Jenks to Polk, June 19, 1847, JKP; Appleton's Journal, June 23, 1847; *Philadelphia Bulletin*, June 24, 1847, and *New York Herald*, June 25, 1847.

12. Appleton's Journal, June 24, 1847; *New York Herald*, June 25, 1847.

13. Appleton's Journal, June 24, 1847; *New York Herald*, June 26, 1847.

14. Appleton's Journal, June 25, 1847.

15. Ibid.

16. *New York Herald*, June 26, 1847; Appleton's Journal, June 25, 1847.

17. *New York Herald*, June 26, 1847; Appleton's Journal, June 25, 1847.

18. *New York Herald*, June 27, 1847; Appleton's Journal, June 26, 1847. The Washington *National Intelligencer*, leading opposition newspaper in the nation's capital, followed the president's progress with passing interest and but intermittent coverage, generally from other Whig newspapers. It carried an excerpt from the New York *Evening*

Mirror on the president's visit to Brooklyn: "His reception was not calculated to give him much satisfaction, for we never saw so large a concourse of people before where there were so few evidences of enthusiasm. The people crowded to see the President, and not to cheer or welcome Mr. Polk." The *Intelligencer* borrowed this gem from the New York *Commercial Advertiser:* "A few ragged, jacketless, dirty boys, an equal number of women with candy stands, a handful of soldiers gathered around a grogshop, five or six others walking about with peonies as large as nutmeg melons stuck in the neighborhood of the fifth button, and sundry loafers, were all that then waited Mr. Polk's advent." Without comment, the *Intelligencer* also reprinted the story of Polk's visit to Brooklyn as described more fully and more favorably in the *New York Herald.* Washington *National Intelligencer,* June 30, 1847.

19. Appleton's Journal, June 26, 1847. Upon returning to Washington City, Polk confided to his diary the following assessment of his relationship with Van Buren: "At New York, as I proceeded North, Mr. Benj. F. Butler delivered me a verbal invitation from Ex. President Van Buren, inviting me to visit him. I declined it, stating that my arrangements, previously made, did not contemplate a visit to that part of the State. I thought also (though I did not say so to Mr. Butler) that if Mr. Van Buren really desired me to visit him he would have written to me inviting me to do so, and that he would not have postponed this verbal message, delivered through Mr. Butler, to so late a period. I considered it a mere act of formal courtesy, which Mr. Van Buren, probably, thought public opinion constrained him to extend to me. The truth is Mr. Van Buren became offended with me at the beginning of my administration, because I chose to exercise my own judgment in the selection of my own Cabinet, and would not be controlled by him and suffer him to select it for me." Milo Milton Quaife, ed., *The Diary of James K. Polk,* 4 vols. (Chicago: A. C. McClurg, 1910), 3: 73–74.

20. *New York Herald,* June 28, 1847.

21. *New Haven Herald,* June 26, 1847, reprinted in the *New York Herald,* June 28, 1847.

22. *New York Herald,* June 29 and July 1 1847; Appleton's Journal, June 28, 1847.

23. *New York Herald,* July 1, 1847; Appleton's Journal, June 28, 1847.

24. Appleton's Journal, June 29, 1947.

25. *Boston Post,* June 30, 1847; Appleton's Journal, June 29, 1847; and the *New York Herald,* July 1, 1847.

26.. Appleton's Journal, June 29, 1847; Polk to Sarah C. Polk, June 30, 1847, JKP.

27. *Boston Post,* July 1, 1847; *New York Herald,* July 3, 1847; and Appleton's Journal, June 30, 1847.

28. Appleton's Journal, July 1, 1847; *Boston Post,* July 3, 1847; and Henry Hubbard to Polk, May 17, 1847, JKP.

29. Appleton's Journal, July 2, 1847; *Boston Post,* July 3, 1847.

30. Appleton's Journal, July 3, 1847.

31. Philadelphia *Pennsylvanian,* July 12 and 8, 1847; *New York Tribune* quotation as reprinted in the *Pennsylvanian,* July 12, 1847.

JOHN S. D. EISENHOWER

Polk and His Generals

IN studying the war between the United States and Mexico (1846–48), I have been struck by certain superficial similarities between that conflict and World War II. In both instances we see initial unpreparedness, public resistance to war, American troops sent overseas prior to hostilities, a roused public reaction when those exposed forces were attacked, initial operations on the enemy's periphery, an amphibious expedition leading into the enemy's heartland, difficult presidential decisions as to who would command, and victory in eleven months after the launching of the invasion.

But all this is a whimsical exercise. The differences are even more significant: in World War II the United States fought with allies against a first-class foe; we suffered severe defeats at the outset; and we annexed no territory except for some bases in the Pacific. But the feature of the Mexican War that I find most interesting is the lack of harmony that existed between the political and military leadership. Whereas the relationships between President Franklin D. Roosevelt, Gen. George C. Marshall, and Adm. Ernest J. King were nearly ideal during World War II, those between President James K. Polk, Gen. Winfield Scott, and Gen. Zachary Taylor were unbelievably bad. That interplay between Polk and his two principal generals will be the subject of this piece. I shall make no effort to present a balanced picture of the whole war.

Actually, the disharmony that plagued the intercourse between Polk and his two main generals came about, I believe, more from the circumstances than from the personalities of the protagonists. Polk, Scott, and Taylor were, to be sure, strong-willed men, consistent with that age of rugged individualism. But I believe that if the line-up had been different—if, for example, Taylor rather than Scott had started out as army general in chief—the clashes, though less dramatic, would still have occurred. Polk (or any other politician, for that matter) would still have felt political pressures for quick restoration of peace. He would still have demanded impossible results, and Taylor would have resisted because the respective roles of the president and the generals were not yet clearly delineated. That delineation, which we associate with the development of military professionalism, would not occur until the Civil War, when the influence of West Point would make itself felt in the higher echelons of the army. The discord was inherent in the times.

This unhappy situation, the antagonism between Polk and his generals, affected the conduct of the war. The unbroken string of U.S. victories achieved from Palo Alto in May, 1846, to Mexico City sixteen months later should not delude us into thinking that the war was well managed from a military viewpoint. It was, I contend, very badly managed, and the United States was lucky to be spared the sort of disasters we suffered at the outset of our involvement in World War II. We were so spared because our armies fought better—and the Mexican high command fought worse—than we had any right to expect. The invaluable contributions of our young West Point officers came largely as a surprise. Without that unexpected bonanza of hidden competence the story of the war with Mexico, at least in the early stages, might have been far different.

But a more important reason for my contention that the war was mismanaged is the fact that some of our victories were close calls and all were expensive in lives. The history books gloss over the fact that from the viewpoint of the participants the Mexican War was the deadliest war the United States has ever fought. During that conflict our forces suffered a cumulative mortality rate of 153.5 per thousand troops per annum, as contrasted with only 98 per thousand for the North in the Civil War.[1] Admittedly, many of these deaths came from disease, but the death rate from that cause was most severe among the poorly clothed, poorly fed, undisciplined volunteers. The fact that we treated those volunteers so shabbily points to one conclusion: mismanagement.

And since our troops were outnumbered in nearly every battle, combat losses were proportionately high. Some of the victims were famous: Henry Clay, Jr., and Archibald Yell, former governor of Arkansas (both at Buena Vista), and Captain Samuel Walker of the Texas Rangers, at Huamantia. Others were less noted, such as Kirby Smith, Philip Norbourn Barbour, and Samuel Ringgold—I could go on.

But then, you might say, "Isn't that what professional soldiers are for, to fight tough battles?" To which I answer, "Absolutely not." We hire our professionals to ensure that we enforce the will of our government at the lowest cost in lives and treasure, not for the sake of glory in equal combat. After all, what general is really looking for a fair fight? Does a policeman give the robber a gun to shoot back? Did General Eisenhower's directive to invade the continent of Europe in 1944 include instructions to give Hitler a fair chance? Hardly. Fair fights are for gladiators, not those charged with enforcing our country's will at least cost. If a country possesses the overwhelming resources the United States enjoyed in the war with Mexico—and then finds itself in "fair fights"—then something has been mismanaged.

What all this boils down to, then, is that our principal antagonist in the Mexican War was ourselves. Supply, transportation, medical care, and sanitation remained woefully deficient throughout the war and caused more delay of the peace than did enemy guns. If that seems to do less than justice to the Mexican army, let us consider the incredible circumstances of calling up the first volunteers. When Zachary Taylor first reported the beginning of hostilities near Brownsville in late April 1846, the news reached New Orleans long before it arrived in Washington. In the excitement the local commander, Maj. Gen. Edmund P. Gaines, set out without word from Washington to organize and equip an army of his own, calling on the governors of Louisiana, Alabama, Mississippi, and Missouri. Before the authorities could remove him from his position he had signed up 12,600 men, over 11,000 of them for illegal six-month terms. He had actually embarked some 8,000 to Taylor's army on the Rio Grande; they arrived after the danger to Taylor had been dealt with. And, once landed, they remained idle for the duration of their (revised) three-month enlistments, returning to their homes, as one authority put it, "without the satisfaction of having fired a shot, their losses by death from disease being 145—but 25 short of those killed and wounded (170) at the battles of Palo Alto and Resaca de la Palma."[2]

Any organization that permits debacles of that sort must be a victim of public neglect. And neglected the army had been. In mid-1845, as Texas was setting out to consider the U.S. offer of annexation, the entire regular establishment consisted of some 8,613 authorized officers and men, organized into eight regiments of infantry, four regiments of artillery, and two of cavalry.[3] That structure was below strength, and desertions were running at about one thousand a year, or about one man in eight. This force was scattered along the frontier in a chain of small posts from Fort Snelling in Minnesota to Fort Jesup in Louisiana, and along the Canadian border as far as Lake Superior. It was designed primarily for protection against Indians, totally inadequate to protect against any other threats.

The problems with that army were not, however, confined to its small strength. Even more important was the fact that it had never been concentrated. Companies of a battalion, battalions of a regiment, regiments of the army, had never seen each other. Thus the techniques of military maneuvers, so necessary for command and control, were unknown to these small units. Knowledge of regimental drill was essentially confined to the instructors and cadets of the Military Academy at West Point. But though the graduated cadets themselves were schooled in regimental drill, no such units were concentrated to practice it. Fortunate we were that circumstances provided General Taylor some eight months at Corpus Christi, from July, 1845, to March, 1846, to whip his small army into an efficient fighting force.

The psychology of the American people at that time was obviously responsible for the weakness in our military structure. The governors of the various states were jealous in protecting their own prerogatives; demagogues preached economy above all else; our people had inherited a prejudice against all standing armies; and neglect of our military establishment was rationalized by the cheerful idea that militia could substitute for a professional army in full-scale war. That idea, welcome as it was, had no basis. Our ragtag militia units had met defeat after shameful defeat in the War of 1812, but that fact had been smothered by sentimental recollection of the defensive battles of Bunker Hill and New Orleans, where entrenchment in strong positions had rendered organization and discipline secondary. These battles, though fought by brave men, had created a mythology that could be used to minimize the need for a respectable military establishment during peacetime.

The Mexican War was, fortunately, not fought by militia, those state soldiers whose legal terms were limited to three months and who were limited by the Constitution to "execute the laws of the Union, suppress insurrections, and repel invasions."[4] Such troops could not be employed for foreign excursions into Mexico. Instead, the war was fought by regulars and volunteers, the latter established by the Congress to serve for a full year or the duration of the war.

A word might be said here about those volunteers. They were, as one might suspect, superior raw material, motivated by a high spirit of patriotism and, as a cross-section of the states from which they were drawn, better educated than their underprivileged brothers of the regular army, 40 percent of whom were foreign born. The volunteers were, by background, allergic to strict military discipline and, when first signed up, were treated like second-class soldiers. Later, however, their combat efficiency rose, and their achievements equalled the results of the regulars.

The volunteer officers, however, were less successful as a group simply because the officer's position requires more training and experience. Some of them, such as Jefferson Davis, had West Point training and were great leavens to their raw troops. Others also had military knowledge and performed well. Most were adequate. But the higher the grade the less likely was the volunteer officer to be up to his job. And as might be expected, the volunteer generals had the most severe problems.

It would have been difficult for men straight out of civilian life to step into general officer positions in any case; but President Polk exacerbated the problem by making his selections for flag rank rewards on the basis of political and personal loyalty. It so happened that his top regulars—Scott, Gaines, Taylor, Roger Jones, and John E. Wool—were outspoken Whigs, and Polk, political animal that he was, seemed actually to believe that these worthies would prefer an unsuccessful, or at least stalemated war, over victory under a Democratic administration. So with that mind-set Polk felt handsomely justified in appointing only Democrats as volunteer generals. And since military competency was a secondary consideration in selection for volunteer general, few in that category ever became wholly fit for the responsibilities they carried. Gideon Pillow was a case in point. Pillow had been Polk's old law partner, instrumental in engineering Polk's nomination for president in 1844. Unfortunately, Pillow was ignorant, rash, and vainglorious. To be fair, he was not alone in his incompetence; he was merely outstanding.

These generalizations regarding the volunteers do not apply to the Texas Rangers, especially those of Col. John C. Hays's regiment, as those unusual warriors were for a large part experienced frontier partisans who had been protecting the western frontier of Texas ever since independence in 1836. Although the Rangers had not been formally organized before February 1, 1845, the five companies then established were readily expandable into a regiment when General Taylor requested troops from the Texas governor in April, 1846.[5]

The accomplishments of the Texas Rangers have not gone unnoticed, I dare say, and one who wrote about them was Walter Prescott Webb. I will not go into detail on them other than to say that in action—as scouts, spies, and cavalry in the attack—they were without peer. As soldiers in camp they were a headache, and as ambassadors of democracy in Mexico they were worse. The governmental policy of trying to win the hearts and minds of the Mexicans through brotherly love somehow did not enchant most of them, and they brought their old grudges with them; their most notable old foe was the Mexican irregular, Antonio Canales, the "Chaparral Fox." The Rangers' proclivity for playing by their own rules often caused an exasperated Zachary Taylor, no cream puff himself, to wish that the Rangers could be replaced by those more amenable to military discipline. But they could not; they were nearly indispensable.

So much for the military situation of the United States in late 1845 and early 1846. Let us now consider the three main personalities we are concerned with, President and Commander in Chief James K. Polk, General in Chief Winfield Scott, and Bvt. Brig. Gen. Zachary Taylor, commanding the bulk of the army in the field.

James Polk, interestingly, was in one way unique, the only American president who ever found himself in personal competition with his principal generals. Washington, during the Revolution, had no single commander in chief to contend with; Madison had no competition with Jackson or Scott; Lincoln had none with Grant; McKinley had none with Nelson A. Miles; Wilson had none with Pershing; Roosevelt had none with Marshall; Johnson had none with Westmoreland. Even Truman's problem with MacArthur in Korea, which resulted in the general's relief, involved the respective roles of president and supreme commander, but it was not a matter of personal competition.

General Winfield Scott. (*Courtesy Jenkins Garrett Library, Special Collections, the University of Texas at Arlington Library*)

General Zachary Taylor at Buena Vista. (*Courtesy Texas Humanities Resource Center*)

But Polk's competition with Scott and Taylor was indeed personal, or at least political, based on the fact that the two were Whigs and that first Scott, and later Taylor, was after his own job. And Polk could never understand the mentality that would cause these men, as professional soldiers, to value their military reputations far above such secondary things as the presidency. Such an idea was beyond Polk's comprehension.

Other factors entered. First, Polk was keenly aware that he was considered an accident in the presidency, condescended to by private citizens and politicians alike. Given his emotional need to be utterly in charge of everything, he not only demanded compliance with his orders but he thirsted for his subordinates' accolades as well. Time and again in his diary we see him recording the approbation of his cabinet. And Scott was obviously insensitive to that characteristic at first. Second was Polk's sincere belief that adequate soldiers could be created instantly by the stroke of a pen, a conviction derived from his strong Jeffersonian-Jacksonian background. And third—seriously—was Polk's size. It seems ridiculous to overplay a few inches of extra calcium in a man's femurs, but one cannot help visualizing little James Polk talking up to a six-foot, five-inch Scott—a striking contrast to a tall, gaunt Lincoln tolerating a little George B. McClellan.

Because Polk found his top military commanders insufferable, he simply tried to replace them to the extent possible. It went further than his habit of appointing friends and political supporters to high rank. Whenever possible, even when dealing with military matters, Polk tended to bypass not only Scott but Secretary of War William Marcy as well. Polk constantly sought military advice from Sen. Thomas Hart Benton, a man of no military experience.

In the light of these shortcomings, it seems as if Polk ran a remarkably intelligent war from a strategic viewpoint. His instructions to Stephen Watts Kearny, Wool, Robert F. Stockton, Alexander Doniphan, and others in the West show a keen grasp of the situation in that region. And to combat the lethargy and lack of organization in the War Department, Polk sometimes supplied some much-needed impetus. Always concerned about details, he even overrode army policies on such concrete matters as procurement of mules and wagons.[6] As the senior partner in a civil-military team effort, Polk was wanting. But as an individual he knew when he was getting results and when he was not. Therefore it was perhaps fortunate that Polk relied from time to time on unconventional procedures and sources of advice. Even as a commander in chief, Polk was not all bad.

Maj. Gen. Winfield Scott, General in Chief of the Army, presented a striking contrast to Polk. Large of frame, outgoing, generous, and egotistical, he had long been one of the most prominent figures around Washington. In contrast to the calculating, introverted Polk, Scott had long suffered a severe case of "foot-in-mouth disease," causing offense by his bluntness. That fault had caused him trouble at times— a court-martial in 1813 for calling his commanding general a traitor, for example—but a certain unwarranted good luck had always prevented his paying too dearly for his indiscretions. His violent criticism of Andrew Jackson during the War of 1812, for example, had brought him no immediate consequences. A resignation he submitted in 1828 had not been accepted. During the Florida War (1837) President Jackson had placed Scott under court-martial for lack of results, but the court wound up congratulating rather than punishing Scott.

As might be expected of someone who had been so prominent for so long, Scott had become a bit of a windbag by 1846, and had he not been a national hero, he would probably have been considered a bore. But his foibles were accepted. That earthy little Whig kingmaker, Sen. John Crittenden, for example, could chuckle at Scott's bombastic letters, defend him to a dubious Henry Clay, and then drop him in favor of Taylor when politics called for it.

But Scott was no buffoon. He was not only brave but competent. He had studied the military profession (an avid reader of the French theorist Jomini) and he had filled difficult diplomatic assignments through his thirty years as a general officer. Thus, while Scott made the error of underestimating Polk during the first stages of the war, he had the qualities to rebound. Scott's greatest military achievement, the one for which we remember him, was still ahead of him.

The third member of this triumvirate, Zachary Taylor, belonged to a breed different from both Scott and Polk. He had spent little or no time in Washington, being instead a lifelong frontier soldier. In person, he and Scott presented a startling contrast. Whereas Scott loved uniforms and panoply—"Old Fuss and Feathers" was his nickname— Taylor, "Old Rough and Ready," practiced informality to a fault. He was once mistaken as an old farmer by some young officers on the way to report for duty. He reportedly wore a uniform only twice during the war—and regretted it both times. In camp he made a habit of sitting at his tent, greeting all visitors courteously, even those with complaints. Before succumbing to the presidential bug, Taylor seemed to be unaffected by personal ambition, annoyed by the sudden adulation that followed his victories at Palo Alto and Resaca in May, 1846. But he was never the country bumpkin that he was sometimes pictured. He read the New Orleans newspapers and digested the significance of everything that was happening in Washington.[7] It is interesting that as a soldier he was revered by his troops, regular, volunteer, and Ranger alike.[8] Certain historians, unsympathetic to the problems he had to overcome, have tended to downgrade him.[9] But his admirers included such outstanding professional soldiers as U. S. Grant, G. G. Meade, and O. O. Howard.

Perhaps the differences are logical: Taylor was an officer who cared for his men, who carried responsibility without flinching, and who fought valiantly and coolly. He had no appetite, apparently, for impressing his superiors. That type of commander is not rare in the army.

I would now like to discuss four episodes in the Mexican War that illustrate the difficulties experienced between Polk and his generals, together with their consequences. These episodes are:

First, the circumstances under which the war began, including Polk's attempt to place the onus on Taylor, and Taylor's reasonably successful passing of the hot potato back to Polk.

Second, the conflict between Polk and Scott in Washington, just after hostilities commenced, and how that brouhaha actually worked to the country's best interest.

Third, how the growing enmity between Polk and Taylor nearly caused a disaster at Buena Vista.

Fourth, how Polk's vendetta with Scott tarnished the glitter of the brilliant military campaign to Mexico City.

The Mexican War began, as most of us are aware, with a skirmish between Mexican and American forces on the left bank of the Rio Grande River, where Brownsville, Texas, stands today. Taylor's army had been sent there, far beyond any Texan settlements at that time, for the purpose of enforcing U.S. claims to the land between the Nueces River and the Rio Grande. Then, when the inevitable clash occurred,

Polk asked Congress to recognize rather than declare the existence of war. But how did Taylor's army find itself in that far-off location in the spring of 1846?

The series of moves that placed Taylor on the Rio Grande was motivated by political considerations, the need to assure the Texans of United States protection, and of support for their boundary claims against Mexico. It will be recalled that the U.S. Congress voted to invite Texas to join the Union during the dying days of the Tyler administration and that Tyler, on his last evening in office, transmitted one version of that invitation to the Congress of the Texan Republic. Polk, on his inauguration, could have countermanded Tyler's act, but he chose to let it stand. The invitation was couched in general terms, and it left the future boundaries between Texas and Mexico to be decided later. But then, while Texas was considering that annexation proposal, Polk gave its prospects a boost by providing the Texans assurance of U.S. protection. That he did by ordering Bvt. Brig. Gen. Zachary Taylor to begin concentrating a force at Fort Jesup, Louisiana, just across the Sabine River. Crossing the Sabine was forbidden, however, as Texas was still an independent nation, and stationing troops on her soil would be a violation of Texan sovereignty.

By June, 1845, the Texas Congress had accepted the annexation proposal and had called a ratifying convention to meet on July 4 at Washington-on-the-Brazos. Until such ratification, Taylor would have to stay in Louisiana.

As July 4 neared, rumors of Mexican invasion caused President Polk to step up the process, and Taylor was instructed to move southward to some port" as may be most convenient for an embarcation at the proper time for the Western frontier of Texas." Taylor was even permitted to enter Texas prematurely if so advised by the U.S. charge, Andrew Jackson Donelson.[10] On June 28, six days before the convention, Taylor and Donelson decided that the time was ripe for Taylor to proceed by water from New Orleans to Corpus Christi. The selection of Corpus Christi as a position was theirs, principally Taylor's: Polk had specified only "the Western frontier of Texas." Little wonder that Taylor began to think he was in business for himself!

Taylor arrived at Saint Joseph's Island, near Corpus Christi, with 1,200 soldiers of the 3rd Infantry, on July 25, 1846. This small contingent was hardly enough to strike terror in a nation of eight million people, but reinforcements would soon arrive. By October, Taylor had 3,554 troops.[11]

In late August, Taylor received a letter instructing him to ask President Anson Jones what additional force Texas could provide him. No provisions for pay had been appropriated, however, and the "amount and description of the force to be mustered into the service of the United States" was left to Taylor's discretion.[12]

Taylor, however—and he can be faulted for this—elected to get along with his small army of regulars, augmented by only a party of Texas Rangers and two companies of Louisiana militia, signed up, as noted, for only three months. At this time, Taylor remained convinced that no war was really in the offing. But right or wrong, he made this decision in late August, eight months before hostilities commenced, and any militia he requested (had he done so) could legally stay only three months. If Polk and Marcy considered him too complacent, they could easily have overridden him.

The logical way to augment Taylor's force would have been to fill out the vacancies in his regular army structure. His infantry companies each contained only about forty privates, but they also had enough officers and noncommissioned officers to allow expansion to one hundred privates each. This sort of expansion could have doubled Taylor's strength.[13] Actually, both Marcy and Scott recommended that increase to Congress during that winter, but their recommendations were ignored. All sides—the executive, Congress, and the field commander—shared in the responsibility for the grave risk that later developed.

Taylor utilized that stay in Corpus Christi well, for during that period he was able to build an army out of the fragments he had received from the frontier. But toward the end of 1845 the hardships of that camp began to outweigh the benefits. The climate on the beach at Corpus Christi had been salubrious at first, but by winter it was becoming uncomfortable and unhealthy. The "northers" kept everyone soaked, and the winds were cold. Further, the law of diminishing returns was beginning to make itself felt regarding the constant drill. So Taylor, as early as October, 1845, suggested a movement forward to the Rio Grande to enforce the Texan—and therefore the U.S.—claim of that river as the boundary with Mexico.[14]

Polk set aside Taylor's suggestion in Washington until he realized that the mission of John Slidell, his emissary to Mexico, was a failure.

Then, on January 13, 1846, he ordered Taylor forward once again, this time to the Rio Grande.

This order was remarkable in that, intentionally or not, it gave Taylor the power to bring on open conflict. In case Mexico should assume the character of an enemy "by a declaration of war, or an act of open hostility," Taylor should "not act merely on the defensive." Taylor was left to judge what was an "act of open hostility" and also whether or not to invade Mexico. At the same time he was authorized once more to make a requisition on the new governor of the State of Texas "for such of its militia force as may be needed to repel invasion or to secure the country against apprehended invasion."[15] Those instructions were contradictory, for they encouraged an invasion of Mexico with militia who, as I have described, could be solely for domestic and defensive purposes, not to be sent outside U.S. territory. Thus, had Taylor crossed the Rio Grande into Mexico, he could have used only his regulars. Not surprisingly, Taylor once more passed up the militia and elected to stick with his regulars—which he preferred to do anyway. It was a great risk.[16]

Taylor's army arrived opposite Matamoros, near the mouth of the Rio Grande, in late March, 1846. For a month the relations between the opposing forces on the two sides of the river degenerated. The Mexican force built up from its original three thousand poor-quality troops to over six thousand first-line soldiers. At the same time the Mexican attitude evolved from correct, cold hostility to open belligerency, with increased guerrilla action on the left (American) bank of the river.[17] Not all the provocation, however, came from the Mexicans. In about mid-April, Taylor, responding to a twenty-four-hour ultimatum issued him by General Ampudia, forthwith ordered a naval blockade of the mouth of the Rio Grande. Because all supplies, both military and civilian, were not cut off from Matamoros, Ampudia's—and later Arista's—hand was forced. A clash was inevitable.

On April 25, 1846, that clash came. A Mexican cavalry squadron crossed the Rio Grande and ambushed a sixty-man patrol that Taylor had sent out to intercept it. Eleven Americans were killed; the rest were captured. And with that action Taylor reported to Washington that "hostilities may be considered to have commenced."[18] The war had begun.

Polk's immediate reaction upon learning of the first armed engagement reveals that he was aware of Taylor's danger. That Saturday evening, May 9, 1846, Ritchie's *National Union*, the administration organ, told the public that Taylor, authorized to call for volunteers, had, unfortunately, "not made his call in time to secure himself against all possible contingencies." But Polk's ploy was too transparent, and his effort to avoid blame for a future disaster would come back to haunt him.

Shortly thereafter occurred the two battles of Palo Alto and Resaca de la Palma, on May 8 and 9, respectively, fought between present Brownsville and Port Isabel. They were small battles, twenty-two hundred men in Taylor's army pitted against Arista's six thousand. We are interested in them only because of the odds against which the U.S. army fought, nearly three to one. They are considered brilliant victories, rightly so, because of the performance of our troops, the superiority of our weapons, and our skill in using them. But these victories were not foregone conclusions. Taylor himself had anticipated the possibility of disaster. Polk had placed Taylor in a risky situation and had then attempted to shift the blame. He had, in the meantime, delegated the power for the general in the field to bring on conflict. Polk's orchestration of the situation had to be either an abandonment of presidential responsibilities or an easy way to bring about war. Maybe it was both.

Although Taylor's message announcing hostilities was sent on April 26, 1846, it had not arrived in Washington by the end of the first week of May. Nevertheless, an impatient President Polk had already decided that he could not "stand in the status quo" any longer and was planning to request a declaration of war.[19] But in the absence of a shooting "incident," his argument for war would be shaky, based only on public feeling against Mexico in general, exacerbated by the recent Mexican treatment of John Slidell. Two of his cabinet, Secretary of State James Buchanan and Secretary of the Navy George Bancroft, were on record as recommending against his course. But when Taylor's message arrived that Saturday evening, May 9, 1846, Polk had what he needed: "American blood has been shed upon American soil!" Nobody could resist that. All of the pending issues, including the boundary dispute, had now become academic.

The result resembled the public reaction to the Japanese bombing of Pearl Harbor. Impelled by motives of patriotism and of concern for the plight of Taylor's little army, men flocked to the banners in more than sufficient numbers. As we have seen, General Gaines was in New Orleans to receive a good many of them.

The reaction in Congress mirrored the sentiments of the country. That body, so divided only hours before, now fell over itself to go the president one better in providing all possible support to the troops in the field. Polk worked over the weekend preparing his war message, and when it arrived at the Capitol on Monday, May 11, the House of Representatives required only a two-hour debate (one and one-half hours of which were spent reading the message) to ratify the existence of war by a vote of 173 to 14. The Senate took a little longer, much to Polk's annoyance, but finally acceded by an even more one-sided vote, 40 to 2. And whereas Polk had contemplated raising only twenty-six regiments, or twenty-three thousand men, to serve six or twelve months, the Congress authorized him to accept fifty thousand volunteers for terms of twelve months or the "duration." It appropriated a sum of ten million dollars. Polk had more resources allotted to him than he desired.

On May 13, the day that the war appropriations bill was passed, Polk conferred with Marcy and Scott. Up to this time Scott had rarely been included among Polk's advisers, but in this crisis military realities, which only he could provide, could not be ignored. The meeting was tense and formal, a sparring match. In outlining his mobilization plan, Scott undoubtedly talked down to a hesitant Polk. And the president, in return, declared Scott's presentation "incomplete" and directed him to return better prepared later in the day. Polk did, however, offer Scott the command of the "forces to be raised," which Scott, of course, accepted.[20]

Marcy and Scott were back at the White House again the next evening. By then, Polk had drawn up his own general war plan, which was simply to "march a competent force into the northern provinces" of Mexico and hold them while a peace was being negotiated. Scott agreed and proposed that the government immediately call up twenty thousand of the fifty thousand authorized volunteers. Polk, though he harbored secret reservations, acceded.[21]

Although they agreed upon war strategy, the lack of mutual confidence between president and general precluded a frank discussion of Scott's exact role during the next few weeks. Polk assumed that Scott,

Secretary of State James Buchanan. (*Courtesy Jenkins Garrett Library, Special Collections, the University of Texas at Arlington Library*)

John Slidell, Envoy to Mexico, 1845–46. (*Courtesy Texas Humanities Resource Center*)

as commander of the "forces to be raised," would move at once from Washington to the Rio Grande. But Scott understood that he could leave when he was ready, after he had organized the first stages of the mobilization. Thus Scott committed his formidable energies to bringing some order out of the existing chaos. The floods of new recruits would have to be organized, fed, paid, supplied with arms, reimbursed for their uniforms, and if possible, trained. Further, Scott was reluctant—sincerely, we must presume—to humiliate Taylor by arriving alone on the Rio Grande without bringing a new, much larger army to justify superseding him. Scott, therefore, pursued his present tasks. Word of Palo Alto and Resaca had not yet arrived.

Within days, Polk became impatient with what he viewed as Scott's delay. Moreover, mounting pressure from southwestern Democrats discomfited Polk. The Democrats resented giving the command of the army to a professed Whig with political ambitions. Apparently in response to these pressures, therefore, Polk and Marcy conspired with Sen. Thomas Hart Benton, chairman of the Military Affairs Committee, to supplement a current appropriations bill with a rider that would authorize Polk to appoint two new major generals and four new brigadiers. These new vacancies would enable him to appoint his own men—they did not have to come from the established army—and thus to manipulate the removal of Scott and Gaines, replacing them by Senator Benton (!) and one other. Taylor was only a brevet brigadier general at the time.

The drafting of such a bill could not be long kept secret, and soon Scott, who had not been informed, "smelt a rat." Unfortunately for his cause, he overreacted and played into Polk's hands by writing a pompous letter to Marcy. Citing impatience "in high quarters" for his departure, he concluded, "I do not desire to place myself in the most perilous of all positions, a fire upon my rear from Washington, and a fire, in front, from the Mexicans." Scott's blunt wording, which DeVoto has described as "insubordinate and injudicious but first-rate prophecy," was just what Polk needed. Piqued already by the success of Scott and others in stalling his bill to appoint new generals, Polk made Scott's letter public. His generals, Polk professed to believe, were actually bent on thwarting his efforts to prosecute the war.[22] Still, Scott was the ranking officer of the army and enjoyed tremendous prestige.

On the evening of May 23, Polk was presented with a possibility for solving his problem. Preliminary news of Taylor's spectacular victories at Palo Alto and Resaca de la Palma came in from New Orleans, bringing with it a new military hero. By Monday, May 25, the information was certain enough that Marcy sent Scott a letter, approved by Polk of course, withdrawing the former offer of the field command and directing that Scott would remain and discharge his duties in Washington.[23]

The rest of the Battle of the Potomac was an anticlimax. Scott's vain attempt to make amends in an abject letter, containing gratuitous and patronizing compliments toward Polk, made no impression. And once more, Scott's provocative wording thwarted his object. His opening sentence was enough: "Your letter of this day, received at about 6:00 P.M., as I sat down to a hasty plate of soup. . . ."[24]

Scott was dealing with someone who gave no quarter. Polk made this second letter public also and stuck to his decision to keep Scott in Washington. The "fire upon my rear," coupled with the "hasty plate of soup," temporarily made Scott the laughingstock of Washington.

But Polk was to sustain humiliation also. Congress, aware of his desire to appoint Benton to one of the two proposed major general slots, authorized only one. So with the wave of popularity now sweeping over Taylor, Polk had no choice but to give that Whig officer the third major generalcy. Benton would have to remain in the Senate.

The upshot of all this childishness, however, turned out to benefit the war effort. The commander in the field, Taylor, remained there. And the general best qualified to organize the new army, vast for its time, remained at his logical post in Washington.

We now come to the third episode, in which strained relations between Polk and Taylor nearly brought about a disaster—and in any case produced only a Pyrrhic victory, the Battle of Buena Vista.

Immediately after Palo Alto and Resaca de la Palma, Taylor's small force of regulars began to receive volunteer reinforcements. The first to arrive represented a chore, not a blessing, because Polk had ruefully decided that the three-month militiamen could not be held for the illegal six months that Gaines had recruited them for. As no battle was in prospect within three months, they were obviously of no potential use. Therefore Taylor shipped them home at the first opportunity. Meanwhile, he crossed the Rio Grande, occupied Matamoros, and for the remainder of May, June, and July, 1846, occupied himself with governing the new territory, coping with disease, and preparing for the move against Monterrey.

A reconnaissance party of Texas Rangers under Capt. Ben McCulloch reported in mid-June that water was insufficient to sustain an army along the route from Matamoros to Linares. Therefore Taylor decided to proceed by way of Reynosa, Camargo, Meir, and Cerralvo.

This move was not easy. River boats able to negotiate the swift waters of the Rio Grande for four hundred miles—only one hundred miles in direct distance—would always be in short supply. In mid-June, however, Taylor occupied Reynosa and in July he sent advance detachments to Camargo. In early August, Taylor himself moved forward.

Taylor was genuinely unhappy with the adulation being heaped upon him back home. He was grateful, of course, that he had won his first battles, but he knew that he had more ahead of him; it was premature for anyone to be touting him for president on the strength of those preliminary encounters. When a delegation from New Orleans came to honor him, Taylor received them in all civility but he was glad when they left. They had, he wrote indulgently, been "on a frolic pretty much ever since they have been here."[25]

Taylor's letters at the time confirm what Scott had been saying all along, that Taylor was tired from the hard life in the field and would have been glad to leave the Rio Grande and return to his plantation in Kentucky. But he also resolved to do his duty.

The stay at Camargo was a low period in Taylor's campaigns, but he could not leave that bad area as soon as he wished because of the slowness in his supply build-up. And while he stayed, disease set in. His army of just over twelve thousand men lost an estimated fifteen hundred, or one out of eight, in the month they stayed there.[26]

In early September, Taylor was finally able to move southward, and on September 20, 1846, his army began the task of reducing Monterrey. At a glance, sheer numbers would indicate that the job was impossible. Taylor had been able to bring only sixty-six hundred troops, half of them new volunteers, and Ampudia, in a fortified city, could marshal some ten thousand. After four days of heavy fighting, which exacted a price of 487 American casualties, he secured possession of the city only by granting substantial concessions to the defeated commander of undefeated Mexican troops.[27] On the morning of September 25, the Mexican garrison was allowed to march proudly out of the city, the officers keeping their swords, the men keeping their small arms, and Ampudia keeping six of his thirty-eight pieces of artillery. But despite these concessions, the prestigious and strategic city was in the hands of the exhausted Americans. A truce, part of the agreement, was to last eight weeks.[28]

In Washington, President Polk was angered rather than elated when he received news of Monterrey's fall. Polk saw the truce as an unnecessary delay of the final Mexican defeat. From the comfort of the White House, Polk wrote, "In agreeing to this armistice General Taylor violated his express orders and I regret that I cannot approve his course. He had the enemy in his power. . . ." The next day the cabinet agreed with his conclusions.[29]

Public jubilation, of course, required Polk to commend Taylor officially; still, he couched his public praise in restrained terms, and Marcy's letter ordering him to recommence hostilities was cold. Taylor, now becoming sensitive, received the letter on November 13, only six days before the scheduled expiration of the truce. In a letter, he concluded that "there is, I hear from high authority, an intrigue going on against me; the object of which is to deprive me of the command; my only sin for this is the want of discretion on the part of certain politicians, in connecting my name as a proper candidate for the next presidential election, which I very much regretted. . . ."[30]

Meanwhile, it was time for Polk to reassess his war strategy. Mere occupation of Mexico's northern provinces was obviously not going to bring peace, and Antonio López de Santa Anna, now reinstated as president of Mexico, had made that clear in late September.[31] Therefore, Polk now resolved to carry the action to a decisive area, down the Gulf of Mexico to Veracruz—and maybe inland to Mexico City.

At first, Taylor might have been selected to command that expedition, but when Marcy received Taylor's truculent reply to his letter regarding the truce, Polk took grave offense. Doubtless influenced by Taylor's growing popularity with the electorate, Polk concluded that Taylor was becoming a worse liability than Scott. But Polk was really happy with neither.

For weeks Polk debated the issue with his cabinet and with Benton. The senator heartily agreed that neither Scott nor Taylor would be fit for such a matter command. To ensure that the undertaking should be directed by none but the best, Benton volunteered to become its commander provided Polk could secure him the rank of lieutenant general so that he could outrank all the rest. Polk accepted this idea with enthusiasm and tried earnestly to promote it among members of Congress, even Benton's old enemy Calhoun. However, the scheme never had a chance.

Finally, as the least of all evils, Polk decided to give Scott the command. After all, Scott had been comporting himself flawlessly. On November 19, 1846, Polk told Scott personally of his appointment. So touched was the general that he nearly broke into tears, and he left the White House swearing fealty to Polk and his administration. Scott did not realize at the time, nor did he until much later, that Polk was still trying to supersede him with Benton even after he had left Washington.[32]

Scott arrived at Brazos Santiago in late December, 1846. At the top of his agenda was a trip up the Rio Grande to Camargo to confer with Taylor. But by now Taylor had worked himself into such a state that he managed to make himself unavailable, whereupon Scott, on his own, transferred the troops he needed from Taylor's army to march overland to Tampico. He left Taylor six thousand men, an adequate force for a defensive mission, but he took four thousand regulars and forty-five hundred volunteers, some of whom were still at Camargo or Matamoros.[33]

Taylor was furious. In his anger, he lowered his stock further by writing accusing letters to Scott, to the War Department (his channel to Polk), to Edmund Gaines, and to Senator Crittenden. Marcy answered sharply on January 23, insisting that his orders must be obeyed.[34]

On February 6, 1847, Taylor received a letter from Scott that resulted in further acrimony. It advised him to pull back from the advanced position he was holding at Agua Nueva, southwest of Saltillo. Taylor considered Scott's letter "tart" and responded angrily that he would not withdraw without an order from "proper authority," by which he meant the War Department.[35] Taylor was in an exposed position, but he refused advice, even orders. His anger beclouded his judgment.

Paradoxically, Taylor's refusal to pull back resulted in his most famous victory, Buena Vista, fought on February 22–23, 1847. Taylor's

General Antonio López de Santa Anna, ca. 1835. (*Courtesy Texas Humanities Resource Center*)

forty-seven hundred men withstood repeated attacks by Santa Anna's army of fifteen thousand in a desperate defensive battle. With an army of volunteers, who had by now become professionals in their own fashion, Taylor calmly handled the battle with his usual competence. At the end of a sanguinary day, the Americans still held the field, and Santa Anna pulled back during the night. That victory, plus the public conception that Taylor was being needlessly sacrificed by Polk, Marcy, and Scott, furnished the ammunition by which the Whigs were to push Taylor the next year into the White House. Taylor's greatest triumph came as the result of a colossal blunder, his worst blunder in the campaigns.

After Buena Vista, one long campaign remained, the invasion of the Mexican heartland by way of Veracruz. It was not only the largest and most daring campaign of the war, it was also decisive.

Tampico, between the Rio Grande and Veracruz, had been abandoned by the Mexicans in the process of scraping up troops to attack Taylor at Buena Vista. About mid-November, 1846, Cmdre. Matthew Perry occupied the town, and it thenceforth served as an embarkation point for the troops Scott was taking from Taylor en route to Lobos Island.[36] From there Scott was ready to sail for Veracruz early in March, 1847.[37]

It would be an ambitious undertaking, and it would be difficult. Speed was essential, for Scott must, everyone agreed, move inland from Veracruz by early April, 1847, to escape the ravages of the *vomito* (yellow fever), so deadly to those alien to the region. In addition, about four thousand volunteers who had enlisted in May, 1846, would soon be eligible for discharge. During this fast-moving operation, a number of inexperienced political generals burdened Scott. Among them were Major Generals Patterson and Butler and Brigadier Generals Pillow, James Shields, Marshall, James Henderson, Franklin Pierce, Persifor Smith, and John Quitman. Some of these, such as Quitman, would perform well; most would learn; a couple, notably Pillow, would be disasters. But to balance the ledger, one of Scott's regular generals, William J. Worth, would also prove to be a mixed blessing.

On March 9, 1847, Scott landed his thirteen thousand men unopposed at a point south of Veracruz. Then, moving inland behind the

"The Army on the March in the Valley of Mexico," by James Walker. (*West Point Museum Collections, United States Military Academy*)

"Heroic Defense of the Belén Gate," by J. Michaud. (*Courtesy Texas Humanities Resource Center*)

city, he laid siege. His patience was rewarded by the surrender, on March 29, 1847, of the garrisons of Veracruz and Fort San Juan de Ulloa. His own losses had been negligible.

The battles that followed present a bewildering list of names, which are of interest only in passing. Let us group them as follows: first, Veracruz, to establish a supply base; second, the Battle of Cerro Gordo, to clear the way out of the lowlands; third, Contreras and Churubusco, to give Scott control of the Valley of Mexico City; and fourth, Molino del Rey and Chapultepec, outposts of Mexico City itself. A three-month stay at Puebla and a truce in front of Mexico City interrupted these phases.

The pause at Puebla was always anticipated, but it was excessive because of Polk's action in diverting three thousand new volunteers, earmarked for Scott, to Taylor instead. But the atmosphere in Puebla was agreeable, and Scott spent the time well, drilling and training. When he left on August 7, Scott's army was up to thirteen thousand again.

Within two weeks of leaving Puebla, Scott had fought the battles of Contreras and Churubusco and the way was open to Mexico City. However, on August 23 Scott granted an armistice. From a military point of view, he obviously should have pushed on, but he needed a Mexican government with which to negotiate a peace treaty. An immediate attack on Mexico City might destroy whatever remained of the Santa Anna regime, and no authority would be left. Accordingly, Scott waited for nearly a month. But his patience availed him nothing because Santa Anna would not consider peace.

Scott renewed the attack in early September. First, he reduced the two outposts of Molino del Rey and Chapultepec. Then Scott entered Mexico City in triumph at mid-morning, September 14, 1847.

Not everything was over yet. Santa Anna, after leaving the city, raced back to Puebla to attack Scott's sick and wounded. An American division stopped him, but Capt. Samuel Walker, at the head of a band of Texas Rangers, was killed in the nearby village of Huamantla. In the streets of Mexico City, Scott was forced to take strong measures for a while—after all, he had to control 180,000 people with an army of 6,000 effectives.

After difficult negotiations, a peace treaty, which accorded with President Polk's objectives, was signed at the nearby village of Guada-

"Heroic Defense of the City of Monterrey," by J. Michaud. (*Courtesy Texas Humanities Resource Center*)

"General Scott's Entrance into Mexico City," by Carl Nebel. (*Courtesy Jenkins Garrett Library, Special Collections, the University of Texas at Arlington Library*)

lupe Hidalgo on February 2, 1848. The last American soldier left Mexico City on June 12, 1848.

Polk and Scott remained at odds personally throughout this campaign. The old acrimony resurfaced, particularly after Scott learned that Polk had tried once more to supersede him with Senator Benton. Although they eventually became allies, Scott did not intially welcome Polk's designated peace negotiator, Nicholas Trist. Nevertheless, that animosity did nothing to injure the actual conduct of the operation. When Polk sent three thousand new volunteers to Taylor instead of Scott, he admittedly caused delays. But that decision, though an honest mistake, was made on March 22, 1847, when Polk was still very much concerned about Taylor's exposed position at Buena Vista. Even though Taylor had won that battle a month earlier, Polk did not find out until April 1, too late to reverse the orders.[38]

The same cannot be said of the unhappy period after Mexico City had been taken. During the campaign Polk had been looking forward to relieving Scott at some propitious time, and his chance came in the spring of 1848.[39] Three of Scott's subordinates—Worth, Pillow, and Colonel Duncan—believed that they, not he, were primarily responsible for Scott's successes. This attitude was reflected in their official reports (a situation Scott handled clumsily) and, worse, in newspaper articles such as one in the New Orleans Delta, signed by "Leonidas," which placed Pillow "in command of all the forces engaged" at Churubusco.[40] The article was duly reprinted throughout the country, including the Washington Union and the American Star in Mexico City. When Scott eventually preferred court-martial charges against the three offenders, Pillow appealed to Polk and Worth to his old friend Marcy. Polk, ever loyal to his former law partner, relieved Scott of command, sent him to Puebla, and placed him, as prosecutor, as a de facto defendant in a court of inquiry. The court continued until after all parties had returned home, Scott being received in triumph much as MacArthur was in April, 1951. The inquiry convened once again in mid-summer, this time located in Frederick, Maryland. It eventually absolved Pillow, who celebrated his exoneration with Polk at a dinner in the White House.[41]

Although the army received Polk's treatment of Scott bitterly, the episode had little lasting effect. Scott commanded the army for another thirteen years into the Civil War. He was also nominated by the Whigs for president in 1852. Taylor was elected president in 1848, and one must feel a twinge of sympathy for Polk as he rode down Pennsylvania Avenue on March 4, 1849, with Taylor as his successor. Polk was, indeed, an exhausted man, whose overwork in office doubtless brought on his untimely death only a couple of months after leaving office.

The story ends there. In summary, President Polk's clashes with his two principal generals, unique in American history, sometimes caused near disaster. Once Polk retained Scott in Washington, the results were positive. The selfishness that caused those clashes was a disservice to those who patriotically risked—and sometimes lost—their lives. They occurred between three good men from the same region of the country, very largely caused by the fact that military professionalism, that attitude which separates the military from the mainstream of American affairs, had not yet come of age. In the lower ranks, the letters and diaries of men like Grant, Meade, Lee, Howard, and others—products of Sylvanus Thayer's West Point—reflect professionalism of a high order. These men would direct both sides of the Civil War thirteen years later. Beginning with them, the separate but cooperative roles of the political and the military during war would be respected. Open warfare between the chief executive and his generals would become the exception rather than the rule.

NOTES

1. Stanhope Bayne-Jones, *The Evolution of Preventive Medicine in the United States Army, 1607–1939* (Washington, D.C.: Government Printing Office, 1968), p. 86; quoted in Thomas R. Irey, "Soldiering, Suffering, and Dying in the Mexican War," *Journal of the West* 11, no. 2 (April, 1972): 285–98.

2. Emory Upton, *The Military Policy of the United States* (Washington, D.C.: Government Printing Office, 1917; first MS, 1881), pp. 201–202.

3. Alfred Hoyt Bill, *Rehearsal for Conflict* (New York: A. A. Knopf, 1947), p. 59.

4. U.S. Constitution, art. I, sec. 8, para. 15.

5. Walter Prescott Webb, *The Texas Rangers in the Mexican War* (Austin, Tex.: Jenkins Garrett Press, 1975), p. 7.

6. Allan Nevins, ed., *Polk: The Diary of a President, 1845–49* (London: Longmans Green, 1929) (hereinafter cited as *Polk Diary*).

7. Edward J. Nichols, *Zach Taylor's Little Army* (Garden City, N.Y.: Doubleday, 1963), p. 30; Luther Giddings, *Sketches of the Campaign in Northern Mexico in Eighteen Hundred Forty-Six and Seven* (New York: Putnam, 1853), pp. 71–72.

8. See inscriptions to Taylor in flyleafs of John R. Kenly, *Memoirs of a Maryland Volunteer* (Philadelphia: J. B. Lippincott, 1873) and Samuel C. Reid, Jr., *The Scouting Expeditions of McCullough's Texas Rangers* (New York: Books for Libraries Press, 1847; repr. 1970).

9. Justin Smith and DeVoto are particularly severe. See Justin H. Smith, *The War with Mexico*, 2 vols. (Gloucester, Mass.: Peter Smith, 1963; orig. Macmillan, 1919); Bernard DeVoto, *The Year of Decision, 1846* (Boston: Little, Brown, 1943).

10. Marcy to Taylor, June 15, 1845, in U.S. Government, *Executive Document #60, House of Representatives, 30th Congress, First Session: Messages of the President of the United States with the Correspondence, Therewith Communicated, Between the Secretary of War and Other Officers of the Government: The Mexican War* (Washington, D.C.: Wendell and Van Denthuysen, 1848) hereinafter cited as *Exec. Dec.* 60).

11. W. A. Croffut, ed., *Fifty Years in Camp and Field: The Diary of General Ethan Allen Hitchcock* (New York: G. P. Putnam's Sons, 1909), p. 197; Upton, *Military Policy*, p. 199.

12. Marcy to Taylor, August 6, 1845, *Exec. Doc.* 60.

13. Upton, *Military Policy*, p. 198.

14. Taylor to the Adjutant General, Oct. 4, 1845, *Exec. Doc.* 60.

15. Marcy to Taylor, Jan. 13, 1846, *Exec. Doc.* 60.

16. Upton, *Military Policy*, p. 197.

17. When the popular Col. Truman Cross was ambushed and killed, the temper of the Americans became far more belligerent, and hostilities became more likely.

18. Taylor to the Adjutant General, Apr. 26, 1846, *Exec. Doc.* 60.

19. *Polk Diary*, May 8, 1846., p. 81.

20. Polk recorded that he had made the offer even though he did not consider Scott "in all respects suited to such an important command." *Polk Diary*, May 13, 1846. p. 90.

21. In his diary Polk called the plan "too ambitious: and claimed that he went along with it only to avoid future accusations of giving Scott less than he believed he needed. Texas, Arkansas, Illinois, Missouri, Ohio, Indiana, Kentucky, Tennessee, Alabama, Mississippi, and Georgia were to provide the volunteers. All except Georgia were west of the Alleghenies. *Polk Diary*, May 14, 1846, pp. 93–94.

22. Scott to Letcher, June 5, 1846, in Mrs. Chapman Coleman, ed., *The Life of John J. Crittenden, with Selections from His Correspondence and Speeches*, 2 vols. (Philadelphia: J. B. Lippincott, 1871), 1: Scott to Marcy, May 21, 1846, in *Congressional Globe*, Appendix, 29th Cong., 1st sess., 1846, p. 198; DeVoto, *Year of Decision*, p. 198; *Polk Diary*, May 22, 1846, p. 100.

23. *Polk Diary*, May 25, 1846, p. 104.

24. Scott to Marcy, May 25, 1846, in *Congressional Globe*, Appendix, 29th Cong., 1st sess., 1846, p. 198.

25. Taylor to R. C. Wood, June 12, 1846, in Zachary Taylor, *Letters of Zachary Taylor from the Battlefields of the Mexican War* (Rochester, N.Y.: Wm. K. Bixby, 1908).

26. Irey, "Soldiering"; Upton, *Military Policy*, p. 208.

27. *Exec. Doc.* 60, p. 10, table B, p. 28, table D.

28. Bill, *Rehearsal*, pp. 156–58.

29. *Polk Diary*, Oct. 11 and 12, 1846, pp. 155–56.

30. Taylor to R. C. Wood, Nov. 10, 1846, in Taylor, *Letters from the Battlefield*, pp. 66–67.

31. Earlier in the year Polk had ordered the U.S. naval squadron off Vera Cruz to allow Santa Anna to slip through the blockade on his way from Havana to Vera Cruz. Polk

had been duped into hoping that Santa Anna would make peace and cede all the western lands that Polk was seeking.

32. *Polk Diary*, Nov. 19, 1846, and pp. 171–72n.; also, Dec. 14, 1846, p. 175.

33. Matthew Forney Steele, *American Campaigns*, vol. 1 (Washington, D.C.: U.S. Infantry Association, 1943), p. 105.

34. Nichols, *Taylor's Army*, pp. 197–98; Coleman, ed., *Crittenden*, p. 272.

35. Taylor to R. C. Wood, Feb. 9, 1847, in Taylor, *Letters from the Battlefield*, pp. 85–87.

36. Taylor was annoyed to read that Perry had represented this unopposed landing as a significant military achievement. Ibid., Dec. 13, 1846, pp. 77–79.

37. Steele, *American Campaigns*, p. 105.

38. *Polk Diary*, Mar. 22, 1847, p. 206; Apr. 1, 1847, p. 208.

39. Ibid., June 12, 1847, p. 243.

40. Charles Winslow Elliott, *Winfield Scott: The Soldier and the Man* (New York: Macmillan, 1937), pp. 567–68.

41. For a complete coverage of this complicated controversy see ibid., pp. 565–84, 588–90.

MIGUEL E. SOTO

The Monarchist Conspiracy and the Mexican War

WITH a very few exceptions, Mexican historians who have dealt with the Mexican-American War of 1846–48 have placed Mexico in the position of a poor victim of perfidious American imperialism and have put all the blame of the conflict upon the United States.[1] For most of those authors, it was the Americans who, knowing from the beginning what they were after, provoked the war and thus took advantage of a weak and devastated neighbor. A number of more recent authors have shown that the problem was not as simple as that. It is a fact that at this time in Mexico, the idea of war with the United States was quite popular. A true understanding of this conflict is still far from being reached and, as one Mexican scholar has suggested,

> The event was traumatic and still is so, because we do accept the loss of territory, the unavoidability of the confrontation and its results, but we can only regret the facility with which the war was won, and the total impotence of the Mexican army at the hands of the American offensive. We do not understand all that simply because we have not made the effort to do so. Historians have insisted upon taking sides with the factions of the period and upon blaming their opponents for the failure. Gómez Farías, or Paredes y Arrillaga. Santa Anna—the favorite villain, the army or the church, are [according to each partisan view] the guilty ones.[2]

The truth is, as has been pointed out, Mexican public opinion and all the various political factions that aspired to or that actually shared in power at that time, had to—willingly or unwillingly—participate in a very hawkish attitude toward the war.[3] Anyone who tried to avoid open conflict with the United States was treated as a traitor. That was precisely the case of President José Joaquín de Herrera. At one time he, at least, seriously considered receiving the American special envoy, John Slidell, in order to negotiate the problem of Texas annexation peacefully. But as soon as he assumed that position, the president was accused of favoring the handing over of a part of national territory; he was accused of treason and was overthrown.

It is interesting that at least one perceptive contemporary analyst of Mexico's political scene, José Fernando Ramírez, not only understood his dilemma but wrote about it in a series of letters later published in a book. He said:

> The key to the riddle is very simple; it is the same by which all the public misfortunes of the last ten or twelve years can be explained. The Texas war has been the excuse for the last revolutions and misgovernments; today it is a weapon that each one of the contenders wants to have [in order] to hurt his opponents to the last extreme . . . [the struggle] will be lost by the first one to speak about peace and for that reason no one wants to express the terrible word.[4]

As David Pletcher revealed some years ago, one of these many hawkish, patriotic factions that aspired to power in Mexico's complex and confusing political atmosphere of the period was one that supported the concept of returning Mexico's government to a monarchist system similar to what it had enjoyed during the colonial era.[5] Lucas Alamán, an outstanding politician and publicist, headed the monarchist faction. Alamán had actually opposed the possibility of war with the United States as late as October of 1845. But a few months later, when he and the monarchists finally came into power, they pushed for the war as hard as anyone else had done up to then. What made Alamán change his mind about an event that would prove decisive and ultimately catastrophic for Mexico? The reason for that change was that Alamán, along with the Spanish minister in Mexico, Salvador Bermúdez de Castro, was trying to encourage General Mariano Paredes y Arrillaga to destroy the current Mexican political system and establish a monarchy with a Spanish prince at its head. Unfortunately, as will be seen, the only way for this ambitious general to achieve ultimate power in Mexico was to support war with the United States.

This study will explore the development of this conspiracy against the republican system and its implications for open conflict between Mexico and the United States.

At the end of August of 1845 the joint efforts of Great Britain and France to avoid Texas annexation to the United States had failed. Then Bermúdez de Castro reported to his superiors in Madrid that the time had arrived to carry out his instructions to help establish a monarchical

Mariano Paredes y Arrillaga, President of Mexico. (*Courtesy Texas Humanities Resource Center*)

government in Mexico, with a member of the Spanish royal family at its head.[6] Minister Bermúdez informed them that General Paredes commanded the only true army that existed in Mexico and was ready to go along with the project. Another important sector that would favor their plan was the wealthy property owners; one more source of support would come from the Catholic church, both from its upper hierarchy and from the rural priests. The picture presented by Bermúdez to the Spanish government was that the "establishment" institutions of Mexican society were hoping that Spain would come to their rescue by sending them a prince who most probably would stop the turmoil the country had experienced ever since independence. In fact, said Bermúdez, what those sectors of Mexican society were calling for was the fulfillment of a previous petition—one that was included in the very document that had provided Mexico with independence: the 1821 Plan of Iguala. Indeed, the first political option proposed in that plan was an invitation to the Spanish royal family to send a member to rule over the new nation.[7] There were more than a few Spanish authorities who still considered this petition in effect.

Lucas Alamán considered that it was time for Mexico to return to the monarchist system or face its own disintegration.[8] Twenty years of instability was proof of the urgent need for some kind of change. It seemed obvious that Mexico should take advantage of Spanish willingness to collaborate in a monarchist project.

General Paredes was an ambitious military officer who had already participated in two political movements, ones that had granted him only secondary political positions. Now, at least in the view of Bermúdez and Alamán, he was willing to play the role of a "transitional" authority while the foreign prince made his way to Mexico. He may well have expected to play a dominant role in influencing the direction of the new monarchist government.[9]

The Spanish government had several reasons for involving itself in the Mexican monarchist scheme. First of all, Spanish authorities were seriously concerned about American expansionism; in its current frame of mind, the United States might not be satisfied with Texas and other Mexican territories, but might move toward Cuba and Puerto Rico as well.[10] Another important motive for Spanish intervention was that there existed the very real probability that the European prince petitioned by the Mexicans would be Spanish, since that had already been suggested in the Plan of Iguala. Spanish leaders were also facing a major political quandary in trying to marry off the young Queen Isabel II. Since they had several candidates and the court of Madrid was playing its options with the various choices to its own advantage, there existed the problem of what to do with the unsuccessful ones. One possibility was to send some of the unchosen to the former colonies in America.[11] Mexico was one of the best of those possibilities. Not the least of the reasons for Iberian intervention was that there were commercial interests in Mexico that several Spanish merchants had expressed in vivid terms to that government. These commercial interests considered that Mexico still had many resources that should be exploited by Spanish people.[12]

Even before receiving an answer from Spain, minister Bermúdez decided that it was time to cooperate with Lucas Alamán. He and the latter maintained a correspondence in the fall of 1845 with General Paredes, who was stationed in San Luis Potosí. From that correspondence it becomes clear that there were some disagreements—some minor, some not so minor—among the plotters. One of the causes for disagreement had to do with a formal declaration of their true goals in the plan to overthrow the current government headed by President Herrera. The issue was over the establishment of a monarchy in its place. Bermúdez and Alamán insisted to Paredes that their objective should be made clear to everyone, so that the various concerned groups would participate and support their movement. They told the general that his manifesto was to be an important one, since it was going to be "read, translated and commented upon in Europe."[13] It seems, however, from the content of these letters, that Paredes was in favor of obscuring, at least for the time being, this important point.

But another major source of disagreement between the various monarchist plotters consisted of nothing less than the possibility of waging war against the United States. Although Alamán and Bermúdez thought that Mexico should avoid an open conflict with her northern neighbor, General Paredes believed that war with the United States was something that could not or should not be avoided. Paredes's fellow intriguers considered his aspirations of recovering Texas as somehow "illusory."[14] It was painful, they admitted, but "the time for this matter has already passed: a military campaign against the Texans alone, [considering] the lack of resources of this country would be difficult: [if the Texans were helped by] the United States, impossible." At the same time that the plotters presented the raw truth to Paredes, they tried to flatter his military ego by pointing out to him that the existence of a "disciplined, numerous and brilliant army" commanded by "valiant and capable officers" was still not enough to overcome the odds against a successful campaign against Texas. Now it was more important to keep other Mexican territories out of danger. It was clear that the prodigious lands of California could be lost in a conflict with the United States. Therefore, it was better to cut the "gangrenous" organ— Texas—in order to save the rest of the body.

Another important consideration that favored the pacifist views of the plotters was a widespread rumor at that time, according to which the Herrera government was ready to receive an American envoy to settle the Texas problem. It was said that the authorities of both countries had agreed to accept the Rio Nueces as the border between the two nations and that the U.S. government had agreed to pay $12 million as an indemnification for that territory. At that time—as rumor reported—the Herrera administration had already sent its positive reply to Veracruz, where the American envoy would soon be arriving. The plotters could naturally assume that the responsibility for the turning over of Texas would fall completely upon Herrera. That event would openly facilitate his overthrow, and then Paredes could use to his own advantage the economic resources obtained in the indemnification. At the same time, the problem of war over Texas would be resolved.[15]

In any event, the monarchist intriguers insisted to Paredes that the only real hope for the future security of the Mexican territories was the establishment of an "inexpugnable" barrier between the two countries: one that would consist in the incompatability of two opposing political systems: a republic in the United States, a monarchy in Mexico.[16]

To these pacifist arguments Paredes presented his own point of view. He considered that if the army under his command did not move northward and show its willingness to fight the American enemy, it would be accused of abandoning its primary duty—the defense of the nation—and dedicating itself to playing politics instead. Then his army, in all justice, could as punishment be disbanded by the government and President Herrera could achieve what was for him a long-term goal: the substitution of the regular army by the civil militias.[17] Even more, if the army that Paredes headed did not show its enthusiasm for fighting the war, then the Herrera administration could proceed in completing the Texas annexation agreement without any obstacle, since it could claim it had no army support for resistance to the final loss of Texas. Thus, it was not convenient politically for Paredes and his army to wait and see what the next move of the Herrera government would be.

Instead, if the army took the initiative in the matter of the war, not only would it destroy all the arguments of the government against it, but also it would appeal to a "generalized opinion" that openly favored the war: such popularity would ensure the final success of their rebellion. Perplexingly, Paredes thought that a "demonstration" of the Mexican army against the Texans would not be enough for the United States to, in his own words, "hostilize" Mexico, and, even less, to take other territories away from her. This Mexican officer thought that the American army would have to think twice before taking a step toward an open conflict; but even in case the Americans decided to do so, "a strong government, with plenty of resources and well administered," could confront the situation with dignity and come successfully out of it. This dignified face of Mexico could be displayed even if the war was not won, since the objective was not to win the war but to "restore the Nation's honor." This achievement could also mean a larger economic indemnification from the United States to Mexico for Texas.[18]

In the end it was going to be Paredes's point of view that would prevail. But the conspirators still had to solve several immediate problems. Their plot was in serious jeopardy because of a lack of resources. Although Bermúdez and Alamán had informed Paredes on October 14 that they would be able to provide him with everything he might need for his military uprising, four days later they reported to him that their financial activities were not proceeding exactly as had been expected. First, one of their agents could not contribute the amount he had offered and they were worried about risking exposure of the plot by seeking contributions elsewhere. They were also concerned that sending the money all the way to San Luis Potosí would endanger the secrecy of their plan. Only if he moved to Mexico City could they give him "twice as much" as he needed. Thus, despite their setbacks, they encouraged his enthusiasm by ending their letter with the exhortation: "To Mexico, to Mexico, to Mexico."[19]

Two weeks later the conspirators were able to make their first major move toward their eventual goal. Acting in conjunction with some moneylenders, they offered a loan to the Herrera administration with the condition that a large portion of it would be sent to Paredes in San Luis Potosí. Presumably, sending the funds through official channels would lessen the chances of disclosure. The government, of course, refused to accept such compelling conditions, because although the money was supposed to be directed to the imminent war with the United States, it was clear that it could also be used by Paredes to overthrow the Herrera government. However, the cash shortage of the Herrera administration was more compelling than any of its security priorities; therefore, after a few days of bargaining between the moneylenders and the government, the latter accepted a loan of about two hundred thousand dollars, of which more than half would be sent to General Paredes.[20] Still, the plotters were to suffer a few days of uncertainty, because although the authorities of Mexico had sent the requested amount to Paredes, it did not equal the amount the conspirators had offered. In spite of the reduced financial support, General Mariano Paredes launched, on December 18, 1845, his long-awaited rebellion.

In the document presented to justify that political movement, Paredes accused the Herrera government of trying to give away national territory by negotiating the cession of Texas to the United States and with that, trying to avoid a "glorious and necessary war." With this accusation and with his army of twelve thousand soldiers, Paredes overthrew the Herrera government within two weeks.[21]

Facing the fait accompli of Paredes's takeover, Alamán and Bermúdez did not have any choice but to change their pacifist views and support their hawkish aspirant. Once they made their choice, however, the monarchist conspirators became strong supporters of the war. They founded a newspaper that at the same time as it was pursuing the establishment of a monarchy, it became a major promoter of the war against the United States. The name of this peculiar publication was El Tiempo.[22] One of its principal arguments was that once the United States had annexed Texas and was threatening the integrity of other Mexican territories, the European powers, which were "the true friends of Mexico," could come—and with all justification—save that much-maligned country from American aggression. Besides carrying out such a regenerative task, the European nations could help Mexico out of its seemingly permanent political turmoil and set up once and for all a respectable and long-lasting authority—one that only a monarch could establish.[23]

In their enthusiasm over the war with the United States, the monarchists went so far as to say that the Mexican army could soon reach the outskirts of Washington and burn down the American capital. They also suggested that perhaps it was the destiny of Mexican Catholics to fulfill the "glorious" mission of freeing all the black slaves that the American Protestants held in the southern states. Thus, the monarchist conspirators thought that with the support of the European powers Mexico would emerge quite successfully from the conflict with the United States.[24]

A source of optimism for both the Mexican monarchists and the Spanish authorities also came from London. Although the British minister of the Foreign Office had demonstrated to the Mexicans his unwillingness to go to war with the United States over Texas annexation, the British maintained that they would confront the Americans, if need be, over the Oregon territorial dispute.[25] Besides, when petitioned by the officials of Madrid for support, the British had also expressed their sympathy for the Spanish monarchist project. Since this scheme not only represented the European monarchist principle of "order," it could also mean a brake in the face of American expansionism.[26]

Thus, the Mexican monarchists and the Spanish government thought the moment was right for European intervention in Mexico against the United States.

One has to ask, however, as to how serious Paredes was about the eventual establishment of the monarchy. What is revealed from his correspondence is that Paredes had been carefully leaving his options open since the very beginning of his involvement in the monarchist conspiracy. The day after Bermúdez reported to Spain that everything and everyone—particularly Paredes—was ready for the plan to take effect, the Mexican general declared emphatically to a political sympathizer that it was impossible to establish a monarchy in Mexico at that time. The very idea of having a Mexican aristocracy was "quite ridiculous." In fact, Paredes insisted that he was a fervent republican.[27]

From then on, Paredes played a two-faced game, saying both to the monarchists and to the republicans that they had his support. Even when the general came to power, he managed to maintain that ambiguous attitude. As a matter of fact, when he was "elected" interim president by a junta of representatives of the various departments of the country, Paredes swore to respect and protect the *republican* institutions.[28] Just a few days later, though, he issued a manifesto—written, incidently, by Bermúdez—in which he declared that no one, not even the army, could dictate to the nation which law it ought to follow. It would only be the soon-to-be established congress that would have the absolute freedom to decide which were the true needs of the country. Thus, if that legislative body considered that Mexico needed a different form of government—a monarchy, for instance—no one would be able to question that decision.[29] It should be pointed out here that the make-up of that body—whose prerequisites for election were designed and written by Alamán—obviously favored those members of society who would most likely call for the crowning of a Spanish prince: the church, the army, and property owners.[30]

During the following months Paredes continued to cater to both sides of this political standoff, declaring himself one day a republican, and the next offering to respect whatever kind of government the new congress would establish.[31]

On March 21 Paredes made one more ambiguous move; he offered to maintain the republican institutions but, at the same time, he offered to respect whatever decision the congress would make in relation to the form of government. This move brought him the support of both republicans and monarchists alike.[32]

That occasion was important also because Paredes expressed the final decision of his government as to whether it was going to receive Slidell; that decision was negative.[33] At that time it looked, from the Mexican perspective, as though war was to be just a matter of time.

Minister Bermúdez recognized the inevitability of war with the United States. For his part, he pushed for the war because he feared that the arrival of an American envoy who could negotiate the problem of Texas peacefully could also be a danger for the positive outcome of the conspiracy. Besides, Bermúdez considered that according to the circumstances, Mexico did not have any other honorable alternative but war.[34] Even more, as he reported to Madrid, the Paredes administration had come to rely completely upon favorable outcomes in the first confrontations with the Americans for its own political survival.

If these complex political moves describe the Mexican dilemma over the problem of possible hostilities with the United States, it would be illustrative to take a close look at the events that led to American participation.

When James K. Polk assumed the presidency in March of 1845, the legal procedures for annexing Texas had already begun. But it was to be his administration that would complete the process.[35] In effect, the political platform that had brought Polk to the White House included precisely a plank concerning Texas annexation, along with one concerning Oregon. The Texans however, expressed their final decision officially on July 4, 1845, when they voted overwhelmingly in favor of annexation. During those days another expansionist option opened up for the Polk administration. That summer, a rebellion took place in California against the central Mexican authorities. Thus that territory also became a possible objective for the annexationist politicians of Washington.

The Polk administration tried to take advantage of this new opportunity during the following months. It sent instructions to the American consul in California and to an extraordinary envoy in Mexico to look into the possibility of the United States' obtaining California by peaceful means.[36] In the first case, the instructions were to convince the Californians to join willingly the American Union. In the second one, however, the American representative was to offer to purchase that desirable territory from the Mexican government. With these actions, particularly the latter, the American authorities set up their immediate goals and in doing so seemed to place upon Mexico the final decision as to whether or not there would be open conflict. But the Polk administration itself was to make a series of impetuous moves that would, in the end, contribute largely to the hastening of hostilities.[37]

The first somewhat reckless move had consisted in the unnecessarily strong pressure, exerted by Slidell, on the government of President Herrera in early December, 1845. This administration had agreed to receive an American representative to try to settle the Texas problem peacefully.[38] At that time, though, it asked Slidell not to enter

Mexico City because his entry might provoke its own overthrow by offering to its opponents a pretext for accusing the president of treachery for favoring the Americans. It petitioned Slidell to wait in Jalapa while it attempted to obtain national support for the negotiations. Slidell, however, chose to go ahead and enter the capital. President Herrera tried to buy time by refusing to receive him on the grounds that he did not have the appropriate diplomatic credentials. But at the same time, Herrera was requesting an opinion from the authorities of the different departments as to whether the government should receive Slidell. As a part of that request, Herrera's administration showed very clearly its willingness to negotiate the turnover of Texas in order to avoid a major conflict with the United States that would surely bring worse consequences for the nation. But, as has been mentioned before, Herrera's conciliatory attitude was sufficient justification for his enemies to overthrow him.[39]

The new government established in Mexico was, of course, the one of General Paredes backed up by the monarchists. It was then that Polk himself took the initiative. Obviously trying to intimidate the new Mexican leaders, in mid-January the American executive ordered Gen. Zachary Taylor to move his forces—about a thousand volunteers— from Corpus Christi toward the Rio Grande.[40] This indeed was a bold and provocative move, since the area between the Rio Nueces and the Rio Grande was, at best, a disputed area.

Finally, in early March, Slidell asked the Paredes government whether he was going to be officially received. After consulting with the Consejo de Gobierno (a consulting body to the government), the Mexican authorities answered that they could not receive him because he did not have appropriate credentials. But the Mexican government also could not agree to negotiate while American warships were anchored off the Mexican coasts and when American troops had advanced to the Rio Grande, an area that was still considered Mexican.[41] It seems clear that under such circumstances neither the warlike Paredes government nor anyone else could accept the possibility of negotiations without receiving a terrible blow to dignity and international self-respect.

As things turned out, it was precisely in that disputed area between the Rio Grande and the Nueces where the first skirmish of the war took place. Polk said at that time that "American blood" had been "shed on American soil," but—as has been pointed out—the ownership of the land was still in doubt.[42]

Even though the monarchist plot was not the direct cause for the war, it was still an important matter that the leadership in Washington definitely considered in their conflict with Mexico. While Slidell was in Mexico City, Secretary of State Buchanan wrote to him:

> Should Great Britain and France attempt to place a Spanish or any other European Prince upon the throne of Mexico, this would be resisted by all the power of the United States. In opposition to such an attempt, party distinctions in . . . [the United States] would vanish and the people would be nearly unanimous . . . the United States could never suffer foreign powers to erect a throne for a European Prince on the ruins of a neighboring Republic, without our most determined resistance.[43]

So, in the event that the Mexican monarchists succeeded in their hopes for a European intervention, the Polk administration would certainly not have stood still and allowed it to occur.

The problem for the monarchist plotters was that the Paredes government in eventually calling for a Spanish prince had come to rely upon the first results of the war for its very survival. As is well known, of course, the first battles of the conflict, which took place at Resaca de la Palma and Palo Alto, were disasters for the Mexican army. As soon as news of these tremendous defeats reached Mexico City, the Spanish minister reported to Spain that the prestige of the Paredes administration had vanished and that it was therefore time to consider the monarchist plan terminated.[44] At the same time, Great Britain settled peacefully the dispute with the United States over Oregon. Thus, once they had become irrevocably involved in the conflict, Mexicans—monarchists and nonmonarchists—had to fight and lose—alone—the war with the United States.

Although Minister Bermúdez considered that the first military defeats suffered by the Mexican army were enough cause for canceling the monarchist plot, not all the Mexican monarchists shared that view. They believed that those defeats were minor battles in a larger war and still kept hoping that Congress would call for European support. In early June the long-awaited Congress convened, but President Paredes, in an attempt to save his government, asked the legislative body to maintain the country's republican institutions. This move was not enough for his republican enemies, who—with at least partial support of the monarchists—overthrew him two months later. That, indeed, constituted the end of the 1846 monarchist attempt.[45]

It is ironic, perhaps, that the peninsular authorities placed such importance on the idea of saving Mexico from continuous political chaos and disorder, when the Spanish government itself was suffering from the same kind of turmoil. Throughout the several months that the Mexican monarchist conspiracy lasted, its major promoter, First Secretary Ramón María Narváez—duke of Valencia—had to resign his position not once but twice. The main reason for these resignations were precisely his differences with Queen María Cristina over the possible candidates for the hand of Queen Isabel II.[46]

As soon as the monarchist project aborted in Mexico, Bermúdez reported to Madrid that his image as well as Spain's were completely "clear" of any suspicion on the part of the Mexicans; even the worst enemies of Paredes continued to maintain a friendly attitude toward him and the mother country. Indeed, there was no immediate request to the Spaniards from the administration that succeeded Paredes to explain their involvement in the monarchist plot. One reason for this reluctance might have been that the Mexicans already confronted the United States in open conflict; perhaps they preferred to avoid another confrontation with Spain at the same time. But in 1848, after the Treaty of Guadalupe Hidalgo had been signed and after a political enemy of Narváez openly denounced the monarchist intrigue, the new Mexican government asked for an explanation from Spain. Although the Mexican officials "could not imagine" Spain's participating in an adventure like the one suggested by that politician, they still wanted to clarify these issues for everyone.[47]

The Spanish cabinet—headed once again by Narváez—answered that it had not been involved in the intrigue at all. Once Spain had recognized the Hispanic American republics, she "would never dare" to attempt any designs against the sovereignty of those new nations. Spain insisted that she was only interested in their continued development and well-being. With this answer, the Mexican government considered the monarchist conspiracy completely at an end.[48]

Although this 1846 monarchist plot failed, it was indeed an important antecedent to the one that culminated with the crowning of Maximilian of Austria eighteen years later. In fact, one of the direct consequences of the war between Mexico and the United States was a growing concern in Europe over stopping American expansionism; the French intervention in Mexico was a clear example of that purpose. In more than one respect, the 1846 attempt foretold the enormous difficulties that a project of that sort implied.[49] But it was not until the French tried and failed disastrously in 1862–67 that Mexicans and Europeans alike would finally be convinced it was not possible to establish a permanent monarchy in Mexico.

At first sight the San Luis Potosí rebellion headed by Paredes might seem, like many others of the period, as a simple political movement that sought to establish its leader in the presidency. A number of historians who have dealt with these years have considered it so. Some others have pointed out what they considered to be the monarchist inclinations of General Paredes. David Pletcher finally demonstrated that the Spanish government stood behind Paredes—before and after his seizure of power.[51]

It seems difficult to believe that Paredes's case would be unique in the complex Mexican political panorama of the period. It would also be logical to assume that there would be other military uprisings or seizures of power that could have had similar elements of foreign intervention, which perhaps are yet to be discovered.

A final word about Mexican monarchism, however, should be mentioned. Mexican historiography views the monarchist ideal as the creation of traitorous and ill-informed men with nearly the same patriotic sentiment that predominates when Mexican scholars analyze the war with the United States. But in recent years the monarchist movements in Mexico have begun to be seen in a more comprehensive and sympathetic light. Edmundo O'Gorman, for example, in his works on monarchism has shown that, even though the monarchist solution implied at that time some kind of foreign intervention in the internal affairs of Mexico, the truth is that Mexican conservatives were not that mistaken in their search for a highly centralized and stable authority.[52] Indeed, the long-term administrations of Benito Juárez—fifteen years—and Porfirio Díaz—thirty years—proved that what Mexico needed at that time was precisely a strong and respectable central authority, one that would unify and control a disintegrative, explosive, and divisive political situation.

NOTES

1. One of the earliest works on the subject is the now classic view of the war from the Mexican side, Ramón Alcaraz, et al., *Apuntes para la historia de la guerra entre México y los Estados Unidos* (Mexico: Manuel Payno, 1848), translated by Albert C. Ramsey as *The Other Side: or Notes for the History of the War between Mexico and the United States* (New York: Wiley, 1850). Even though these authors point out the prudence of the Herrera administration and its inability to solve the problem peacefully, they blame the United States for provoking the war.

One purpose of books published in the centennial of the war was to put all the blame upon the American aggressor. Examples are Vicente Fuentes Díaz, *La intervención norteamericana en México* (Mexico City: Imprenta Nuevo Mundo, 1947); José Fuentes Mares, *Santa Anna: Aurora y ocaso de un comediante* (Mexico City: Editorial Jus, 1949). More recent exponents of this view are Gastón García Cantú, *Las invasiones norteamericanas en México* (Mexico City: Era, 1974 [1971]); and Manuel Medina Castro, *El Gran Despojo, Texas, Nuevo México, California* (Mexico City: Diógenes, 1980 [1971]). Both books have been printed several times in the last few years, an indication of the enormous popularity of their condemning view.

2. Josefina Vázquez, *Mexicanos y norteamericanos ante la guerra del 47* (Mexico City: Secretaría de Educación Pública, 1972), pp. 41–42.

3. Gene Brack, *Mexico Views Manifest Destiny, 1821–1846: An Essay on the Origins of the Mexican War* (Albuquerque: University of New Mexico Press, 1975); Jesús Velasco Márquez, *La guerra del 47 y la opinión pública, (1845–1848)* (Mexico City: Secretaría de Educación Pública, 1975).

4. José Fernando Ramírez, *México durante su guerra con los Estados Unidos*, in *Documentos inéditos o muy raros para la historia de México*, ed. Genaro García (Mexico City: Porrúa, 1974 [1905]); Elliot B. Scherr, trans., and Walter Scholes, ed., *Mexico During the War with the United States* (Columbia: University of Missouri Press, 1950).

5. David M. Pletcher, *The Diplomacy of Annexation: Texas, Oregon and the Mexican War* (Columbia: University of Missouri Press, 1973), p. 358.

6. Bermúdez de Castro to Primer Secretario del Despacho de Estado [First Secretary], Mexico City, Aug. 28, 1845, dispatch 109, folio 1, *Memorandum*. All the reports of the Spanish minister to his government and the responses from the Spanish authorities to their minister related to the monarchist conspiracy are summarized in a *Memorandum* dated Feb. 17, 1846, which refers to several documents whose dates vary from August of 1845 to June of 1848. The *Memorandum* is located in legajo 5968, caja 1, of the Archivo Histórico Nacional in Madrid, Spain. I owe the finding of this document to David Pletcher's *Diplomacy of Annexation*, p. 358. Currently there are parallel efforts to both countries to publish simultaneously the diplomatic correspondence related to the monarchist project: by Antonio Martínez Báez in Mexico and Jaime Delgado in Spain.

7. The Plan of Iguala is in Felipe Tena Ramírez, *Leyes fundamentales de México* (Mexico City: Porrúa, 1973), pp. 114–15.

8. José C. Valadés, *Alamán, estadista e historiador* (Mexico City: Universidad Nacional Autónoma de México, 1977, [1938]); Moisés González Navarro, *El pensamiento político de Lucas Alamán* (Mexico City: El Colegio de México, 1952). José María Gutiérrez de Estrada, *Carta dirigida al Escmo, Sr. Presidente de la República . . .* (Mexico City: Print of Ignacio Cumplido, 1840).

9. Paredes was a creole born in Mexico City in 1797 and he—as many creoles—had

fought in the war of Independence on the Spanish side; finally, he had recognized the Plan of Iguala and was incorporated into the "Three Guarantees Army," which culminated in independence from Spain. He opposed the proclamation of Iturbide as emperor of Mexico, and from then on he continued his climb in a military career. In 1841, as a reward for his participation in the rebellion that culminated with the approval of the Bases de Tacubava, he was raised to the rank of brigadier general; in 1844 Paredes was one of the leaders in the overthrow of Santa Anna; see Alberto María Carreno, *Jefes del ejército mexicano en 1847: Biografías de Generales de División y de Brigada . . .* (Mexico City: Impr. de la Secretaría de Fomento, 1914), pp. 35–37; Genaro García, *El General Paredes y Arrillaga, su gobierno en Jalisco, sus movimientos revolucionarios . . .* (Mexico City: Librería Bouret, 1910), pp. 55–56.

10. This fear of the Spanish proved correct some time later, as the Polk administration also considered the possibility of annexing Cuba; see Pletcher, *The Diplomacy of Annexation*, pp. 571–75.

11. [First Secretary to Bermúdez], Madrid, Jan. 2, 1846, no number, *Memorandum*. The candidates to marry the queen were the Count of Montemolín (son of D. Carlos), the counts of Aguirre and Trápani (favorite of María Cristina), and the infants D. Enrique and D. Francisco de Asís. The last one was the winner.

12. [First Secretary to Bermúdez], Madrid, Oct. 31, 1845, folio 2, *Memorandum*.

13. In delineating the steps taken by the conspirators in Mexico I have relied upon a series of letters in the private Collection of Mariano Paredes y Arrillaga held at the Benson Latin American Collection of the University of Texas at Austin. Most are unsigned. The handwriting used in these letters is somewhat peculiar, very definitely neither that of Alamán or Bermúdez, at least, not their normal handwriting. However, through their content it is possible to identify their authorship—the Spanish minister and the Conservative thinker Alamán. [Alamán and Bermúdez to Paredes], Mexico, Oct. 18, 1845, Mariano Paredes Correspondence, García folders 143–44, leaf 370.

14. Ibid.

15. [Alamán and Bermúdez to Paredes], Mexico, Oct. 14, 1845, PGF 143–44, leaf 358.

16. [Alamán and Bermúdez to Paredes], Mexico, Oct. 18, 1845, PGF 143–44, leaf 370.

17. [Mariano Paredes y Arrillaga], "Objeciones," [to Alamán and Bermúdez], n.d., PGF 148, leaf 251. I owe the discovery of this document to Prof. Josefina Vázquez, to whom I here express my gratitude.

18. Ibid.

19. [Alamán and Bermúdez to Paredes], México, Oct. 18, 1845, PGF 143–44, leaf 370.

20. [Alamán and Bermúdez to Paredes, Mexico], Nov. 1, 1845, PGF 143–45, leaf 425. The moneylenders were headed by Lorenzo Carrera, a Spanish merchant who—according to Bermúdez—was the only person, besides Alamán, who knew of their plans to overthrow Herrera. For more details of the loan see Lorenzo Carrera to Paredes, Mexico City, Nov. 8, 1845, PGF 143–45, leaf 448.

21. "Plan de San Luis Potosí," *Colección de las leyes fundamentales que han regido a la República Mexicana* (Mexico City: Print of Ignacio Cumplido, 1857), pp. 265–70.

22. Bermúdez to First Secretary, Mexico City, Jan. 29, 1846, dispatch 190, folio 15, *Memorandum*; "Prospectus" of *El Tiempo*, n.d., Jan. 1846.

23. "Parte Política" [editorial], "Nuestra profesión de fe política," *El Tiempo*, Feb. 12, 1846; "Parte política," ibid., Feb. 8, 1846.

24. "Parte política," ibid., Feb. 5, 1846; "Parte política. La república y la monarquía. A *La Reforma*," ibid., Feb. 6, 1846; "Cuestión del Oregón," ibid., Feb. 10, 1846.

25. Antonio de la Peña y Reyes, ed., *Lord Aberdeen: Texas y California* (Mexico City: Secretaría de Relaciones Exteriores, 1925), p. 18.

26. [Spanish Representative in London to First Secretary], London, Mar. 20, 1846, folio 20, *Memorandum*.

27. Paredes to Joaquín Angulo, [San Luis Potosí], Aug. 29, 1845, Mariano Otero Correspondence, Biblioteca Nacional in Madrid, Spain (microfilm at the Benson Latin American Collection, University of Texas at Austin), 1842–1846, 6852, f. 417.

28. *Diario de Gobierno*, Jan. 4, 1846; Carlos María de Bustamante, *El nuevo Bernal Díaz del Castillo o sea historia de la invasión de los angloamericanos en México* (Mexico City: Secretaría de Educación Pública, 1949 [1848]), p. 94.

29. Paredes, "Manifesto to the Nation," Mexico City, Jan. 10, 1846, printed in *El Tiempo*, Jan. 25, 1846; Bermúdez to First Secretary, Mexico City, Jan. 29, 1846, dispatch 190, folio 15. *Memorandum*.

30. Bermúdez to First Secretary, Mexico City, Jan. 29, 1846, dispatch 190, folio 15, *Memorandum*; Mexico, Ministerio de Relaciones Exteriores, Gobernación y Policía, *Convocatoria*, Jan. 27, 1846, *Colección de leyes y decretos publicados desde el lo de energo, Ed. del Constitucional* (Mexico City: Imprenta del Palacio, 1851), pp. 316–52.

31. A good example of that double attitude of Paredes was his request to the governor of San Luis Potosí to deny in the press of that department that his administration was involved in any way with the monarchists; see José María Flores to Paredes, San Luis Potosí, Feb. 25, 1846, PGF 144–43, leaf 347.

32. Paredes, "Manifesto to the Nation," Mexico City, Mar. 21, 1846, printed in *Diario de Gobierno*, Mar. 25, 1846, *El Republicano*, Mar. 29, 1846; *El Tiempo*, Mar. 27, 1846.

33. Paredes, "Manifesto to the Nation."

34. Bermúdez to First Secretary, Mexico City, Mar. 29, 1846, dispatch 220, folio 23, *Memorandum*.

35. Charles Sellers, *James K. Polk, Continentalist: 1843–1846* (Princeton, N.J.: Princeton University Press, 1966), p. 67.

36. James Buchanan to Thomas O. Larkin, Washington, Oct. 18, 1845, Larkin, *The Larkin Papers: Personal, Business and Official Correspondence of Thomas Oliver Larkin, Merchant and United States Consul in California*, 10 vols., ed. George Hammond (Berkeley: University of California Press, 1951–1964), 4: 44–47; "Instructions," Buchanan to John L. Slidell, Washington, Nov. 10, 1845, *The Complete Works of John Buchanan, Comprising Speeches . . .* , 12 vols. (Philadelphia and London: n.p., 1909), 6: 294–306.

37. The possible participation of President Polk in the "intrigue" to manufacture a war with Mexico through his officer Robert F. Stockton in Texas in the spring of 1845 is now rejected by historians, but his eventual participation in the rebellion of the "Bear Flag" in California is still a subject of debate among his biographers.

At any rate, there is little doubt that Polk was willing to use whatever methods were at hand to achieve his goals. Examples in the war with Mexico were his authorization to James Maggofin to bribe the governor of New Mexico, Manuel Armijo, to avoid open confrontation, and to Antonio López de Santa Anna to return to Mexico for the purpose of ending hostilities. Pletcher, *The Diplomacy of Annexation*, pp. 431, 445; Seymour Connor and Odie Faulk, *La guerra de intervención, 1846–1848: El punto de vista norteamericano* (Mexico City: Diana, 1975), p. 85. The original title of this book is *North America Divided* (New York: Oxford University Press, 1971).

38. John Black to Buchanan, Mexico City, Oct. 17, 1845, in Carlos Bosch García, *Material para la historia diplomática de México. (México y los Estados Unidos), 1820–1848* (Mexico City: Universidad Nacional Autónoma de México, 1951), p. 534.

39. Ministerio de Relaciones Exteriores, Gobernación y Policía, "Circular," Dec. 11, 1845, in Antonio de la Peña y Reyes, *Algunos documentos sobre el Tratado de Guadalupe Hidalgo y la situación de México durante la invasión americana* (Mexico City: Secretaría de Relaciones Exteriores, 1930), pp. 3–26.

40. Sellers, *James K. Polk, Continentalist*, p. 400; Pletcher, *The Diplomacy of Annexation*, p. 364.

41. Slidell to the Mexican Minister of Foreign Relations, Joaquín Castillo y Lanzas, Jalapa, Mar. 1, 1846, William R. Manning, *Diplomatic Correspondence of the United States: Inter-American Affairs, 1831–1860*, 12 vols. (Washington, D.C.: n.p., 1932–1939), 8: 814–15; see also *Diario de Gobierno*, Mar. 25, 1846.

42. Pletcher, *The Diplomacy of Annexation*, p. 385.

43. Buchanan to Slidell, Washington, Mar. 12, 1846, in Manning, *Diplomatic Correspondence*, 8: 192.

44. Bermúdez to First Secretary, Mexico City, May 29, 1846, dispatch 253, folio 27, *Memorandum*.

45. *El Tiempo*, May 23, 25, and 27; June 7, 1846; for the opposition of the monarchists to Paredes, see *El Republicano*, June 10, 1846.

46. Jerónimo Bécker, *Historia de las relaciones diplomáticas de España durante el siglo XIX*, 3 vols. (Madrid: n.p., 1923), 2: 101; *Diccionario de Historia de España*, 2 vols., Madrid: Revista de Occidente, 1952), 2: 627.

47. [Speech of Salustiano Olózaga]. Session of Dec. 1, 1847, Madrid, *Diario de las sesiones de Cortes, Congreso de los diputados, Legislatura de 1847 a 1848* [Nov. 15, 1847–Mar. 26, 1848], vol. 1 (Madrid: Print Viuda e Hijos de J. Antonio García, 1877), p. 200; [Mexican Minister in Madrid to Spanish Minister of Foreign Relations], Madrid, June 29, 1848, folio 37, *Memorandum*.

48. [Spanish Minister of Foreign Relations to Mexican Ambassador], Madrid, July 2, 1848, [without classification], *Memorandum*.

49. Miguel Soto, "The Monarchist Conspiracy in Mexico, 1845–1846" (Ph.d. diss., The University of Texas at Austin, 1983), pp. 259–63.

50. Enrique de Olavarría y Ferrari, *México independiente*, in Vicente Riva Palacio et al., *México a través de los siglos*, 5 vols. (Mexico City–Barcelona: Ballestá y Cía., n.d.); José Ramón Malo, *Diario de sucesos notables*, ed. Mariano Cuevas (Mexico City: Patria, 1948).

51. Pletcher, *The Diplomacy of Annexation*, p. 358.

52. Edmundo O'Gorman, *La supervivencia política novohispana: Reflexiones sobre el monarquismo mexicano* (Mexico City: Fundación Cultural Condumex, 1969 [1967]).

DOUGLAS W. RICHMOND

Andrew Trussell in Mexico: A Soldier's Wartime Impressions, 1847–1848

As a hot-blooded young volunteer in his twenties, Andrew Trussell left his native Mississippi to fight in Mexico. Although there seems to be no indication that he experienced the combat that he so ardently desired, Trussell turned out to be a perceptive observer of life in Mexico. Nineteenth-century attitudes about nature are reflected in his comments about geography, camp life, and valor. The strain of family problems and personal anxieties rise to the surface. The fifth letter even alludes to censorship. Particularly pervasive are descriptions of brawling troops and the problem of discipline. Not only does Trussell provide a vivid account of the nature of soldiering in the 1840s, but his comments upon the Mexican reaction to U.S. occupation are somewhat startling. Some of what Trussell has to say brings to mind the controversy in France concerning 1940s collaboration with the Germans that became a prominent theme in French cinema during the 1970s.

Trussell was an intelligent officer, but he could not spell very well and his tendency to use the wrong case for virtually every other word presented editing problems. Rather than burden the narrative with one *sic* after another, I have simply altered the language slightly by putting Trussell's writing into modern usage. I have added words in brackets in lines where something was lacking or appropriate. The eight letters used in this selection vary in quality. Three are reproduced in their entirety while the other five have been reduced in order to spare the reader from uninteresting as well as repetitive details.

1. Andrew Jackson Trussell to James M. Trussell, Buenavista, Mexico, June 6, 1847. The University of Texas at Arlington Library, Special Collections, Arlington, Texas, Trussell Collection (hereinafter cited as TC), box 1, folder 3.

Dear brother,

I again take the pleasure of dropping you a few lines to let you know that I am still in the land of the living and that I am enjoying good health at this time. I hope that these few lines may find you and your family and the balance of the connection well. My feet are somewhat sore from a march of sixty five miles. We left Walnut Springs, 6 miles from Monterrey. On the 26th of May, we stopped one day on the road and we landed here on the 30th and on that day I received the first letter you wrote to me. . . . We have, I believe, got clear of the desperate complaints of small pox. There were 22 of our company who had the small pox. At one time there were 84 of this regiment in small pox hospital but fortunately I did not have it (although it) marked some of our boys very much. The health of our company is improving some. There are only 11 of our company on the sick list. We only number 49 commissioned and non-commissioned officers and privates. There are only 38 privates now in our company. When we left Vicksburg we numbered 90 men. You can see by this how we have suffered. We have discharged 8 men and I think there are two or three that will get a discharge. There are some that would like to get a discharge if they could. As to my part, I am very well satisfied if I can keep my health. We are camped now where the First Mississippi Regiment was camped at the time of the Battle of Buenavista. It is seven miles from here to Saltillo. This country is perfectly clear of timber and we have to haul our wood from fifteen to eighteen miles and then it is green pine trees. There is not a bush in fifteen miles of here with the exception of three small trees that stand where the battle was fought. There are a great many dead Mexicans lying about here. The Mississippians have sent and taken up several of the officers that were killed here and some of the privates have been taken up and taken back to the [United] States. The Ohioans are here now taking up some of their officers and privates and [have] taken them home to bury them. . . . Nature has done more to fortify that place for the Mexicans than artillery could do. . . . Wheat is raised in abundance. This is a fine wheat country here. I think the valley, as we came up, was beautiful, the beautiful streams running through the valleys. The Mexicans can run the water anywhere they want to. I believe they could run the water up the side of the mountain.

It is currently reported and generally believed that we will have [to] fight here on the same ground where the battle was fought [on the] 22nd and 23rd of February. It is reported that Santa Anna is retreating from General Scott and he has found that there are but few troops here. He thinks that he would like to win one battle if he could. I think we will fight in a few days or rather I hope we will have a brush. General Taylor is at Monterrey or near there but he will be up here in a short time with what troops he has got with him. [With] what troops is under General Wool here and what is under General Taylor at Monterrey, we can raise about 3,000 or 3,500 men [and then] we will be able for [fighting] fifteen thousand of the Mexicans. We would like for General Taylor to come up for General Wool is very sour, he is one of the tightest men you ever saw. The men don't like Wool.

The only good thing we have here is the water. These are the best springs here that I have ever seen. The springs broke up right in the valleys. Saltillo is not a very large place [but] it has one of the finest churches that I ever saw. You wrote [that] you wanted to know if I wanted to remain in the army. I think I would like to remain if I could get the situation that I would like. . . . I enclose [for] you a rose that grew in General Arista's garden. His garden is one of the beautifulest sceneries that I ever saw. I only send this just to let you say that you have saw a rose of Arista's. I wish you would send me a newspaper for I would be very glad to see a paper from the States. . . . General C. M. Price has gone home and Colonel [Jefferson] Davis returned yesterday from the States. I have nothing more but remain your affectionate brother.

2. Andrew Trussell to E. M. Eubanks, Buenavista, Mexico, July 10, 1847. TC, box 1, folder 3.

Dear friend,

After acknowledging the receipt of yours of the 6th of June, I in haste comply with your request so far as capable. There is nothing of interest to write from the seat of the war. The 2nd Mississippi Riflemen, to which I belong, is now encamped several miles southwest from Saltillo in the valley with the Virginia and North Carolina regiment of volunteers, and seven miles east of the pass. The health of the regiment is now pretty good but I assure you that if ever poor volunteers suffered with affliction, it has been the 2nd Mississipians. We have had nearly as many plagues among us as was inflicted on the pharaoh. It has cost Mississippi the life of many a brave son and good citizen. We were first taken in New Orleans and while tossed to and fro on the mighty billows of the gulf for thirty-two days, many a brave and proud spirit found a watery grave and several more have been buried in Mexican soil if I may so term it.

We reached Monterrey on the 6th of April where we stayed until the 27th of May. Monterrey is a large town, but like all Mexican towns and villages, of mud and with flat roofs surrounded by lofty mountains on the south, west, and north. I think it is one of the most beautiful sceneries my eyes have behold. When we left there for this place, we started in between two mountains and remained between them. Yet the road from the former to the latter place runs between two lofty chain of mountains, up a rich valley and a well watered one, which is seldom the case in Mexico. We cross[ed] the thin[ly] connected pass about half way between the two places. I have not seen a tree with the exception of a few shade trees. . . . Saltillo is not as large as Monterrey but built out of [the] same kind of materials and the same plan. The distance is 60 miles from the latter to the former and its 20 miles from here to Agua Nueva, where is the first visible break in the chain of mountains from Monterrey. And [for a] distance of nearly 100 miles, the valley continues on to the right and left with some beautiful green in the direction of San Luis Potosi. We have to haul our wood 20 miles [in order] to cook with [it].

We have a great style of cooking anyway and a variety of dishes. If you call salt pork and beef anything, that is principally all we get with the exception of what we can get from the Mexican market such as pies, Hoosier bread, pan de maiz corn bread, pan de harina flour bread, milk and sometimes carne de puerco fresh pork. About ten days back we were in daily expectation of a battle at this place. Rumors ran high for several days of a fight. The Mississippi boys were the keenest men for it to come. . . . We had a glorious 4th [and] we enjoyed the day finely. Officers and privates, there being no distinction, the boys had full sway. They could not have anyway if it had been necessary. But our commander, General Wool, told us to enjoy the day the best way we

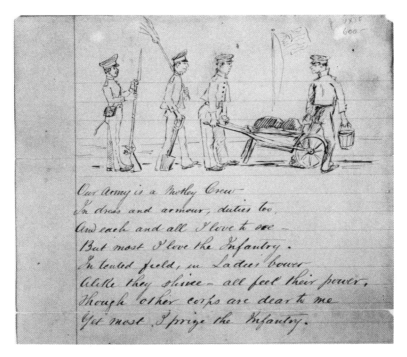

Verse and sketch of the war. (*Courtesy Texas Humanities Resource Center*)

"A Camp Washing Day." (*Courtesy Texas Humanities Resource Center*)

thought proper. The day was celebrated by the whole division turning out together and the firing of thirty rounds of cannon by the artillery. It was a grand scenery.

There will be no movement of this division of the army until the middle of August. I think [that] the impression is we will march on San Luis Potosí. My health is very good at this time. I have been very sick since we got to this place but for the last three weeks it has improved very much and I think I can stand Mexico very well. The weather here is more like October weather is than it is like July. . . .

N.B. Since writing the above, there has come in from a town called Parras [Coahuila] one hundred miles south west of here express stating that there is a body of Mexicans advancing on that place about five hundred strong to burn the place and drive off the stock and to let off the water out of the tank [in order] to prevent General Wool's advance to San Luis Potosí. General Wool started three companies today of the Texas Rangers and some dragoons to meet them and I expect they will have a little fandango, as the Mexicans call battle. The North Carolinans have a disease called the black lung that proves fatal to them. There is not a day but we hear the muffle[d] drum and seeing the regiment at least paying the last respects to a fellow soldier. I must close to be in time for the express which leaves immediately for Monterrey in haste.

3. Andrew Trussell to James Trussell, Buenavista, Mexico, October 26, 1847. TC, box 1, folder 3.

Dear brother,

I again take the opportunity of writing to you [and] to inform you of matters and things in general. As to my health, it is not good, but the health of the regiment is much better than it has been since we started from Vicksburg. Captain Daniel [and] myself are still unwell. The weather is very cool here at this time. We have elected our Colonel and Lieutenant Colonel . . . [detailed description of officer elections follows, complete with runoffs and withdrawals]. . . . we had a great excitement about the election. I expected we would have some fighting but it has passed off so far. But I expect we will have some yet. . . . A few days before the election, [John A.] Wilcox [and] Lieutenant [?]

Amyx had a difficulty but Lieutenant Amyx was under arrest and Wilcox refused to fight him a duel until he was relieved. . . .

About one month ago the Mexicans at a ranch about one mile from our camp killed two men at night and when the news reached camp it, as you know, created a great excitement. Amyx and some ten or fifteen privates of the regiment took their guns and started to the place where the murder was done and finding none of the Mexicans there that done it, he and the men followed the Mexicans over the mountains some fifteen or eighteen miles from camp. But finding none of the Mexicans, he returned next morning and General [Robert] Wood had him arrested and the sentence of the court martial was read out on dress parade yesterday evening. It was that he should be reduced from rank for three or four months and his pay stopped for the same time. Lieutenant Amyx is a good officer and a gentleman. He is First Lieutenant of Capt [A.] McWillie's company. He was tried by regular officers and they hate volunteers as they do the devil and there is no love lost, for the volunteers hate them.

Captain Buckley has resigned and is going home in a few days. Captain McWillie is going home on furlough. Major [?] Price started home last Sunday. One of the Mexicans that helped kill them two men was hung on the 18th inst. General Wood has just left for Monterrey to take General Taylor's place. I understand General Taylor is going home. Colonel [?] Hamtramic of the Virginia Regiment has command of this post. There are three regiments of volunteers of us here and some few dragoons and two batterys of Shermans. There is great talk of peace here now among the troops and the Mexicans say peace is made but we have heard this so often that I don't believe it . . . you heard at Marion that I had resigned my office as Lieutenant. This is not so nor I don't expect to resign. I wish you would get me the appointment of Lieutenant in the regular army if you can. . . .

4. Andrew Trussell to James Trussell, Buenavista, Mexico, November 4, 1847. TC, box 1, folder 3.

Dear brother,

I have just received your letter dated Sept. 28th and 30th and it has given me much dissatisfaction to hear of you being hurt and by such scamps as Riley and Dan Davis. And to think I am here in Mexico so far from you. I wish I had been with you on that day but it was so that I was here. But I hope and trust in him who created all things that he will spare me till I return to that country and if I ever should, I will see some of them [scoundrels]. I would start home tomorrow but it is reported here now that General [Edmund P.] Gaines is on his way here from the mouth of the river with two regiments and that we will move on to San Luis Potosí. If this be true, I want to go with the army. And should this be the case, I will return in time for the damn scoundrels. All I ask of you is to let the goddamn scoundrels be till I return if I should be so lucky as to live to get back. For it will only be a breakfirst spree for me and some of my friends that is with me. And these is my friends for they have been tried in places where a man can tell whether men are his friends or not. It is true I have four or five enemies in the whole regiment, but they are afraid to say any thing. I believe I have the friendship of every officer in the regiment except one or two and they haven't many friends here and the privates are all my friends except old Jim Cook and one other Jim don't like [me] because I whipped him one day for cursing brother John. . . .

Lieutenant Lauderdale of Lowns County has gone recruiting and he told me he would call on you while he is there. He wants to get some recruits in Lauderdale and Newton counties. Captain Daniel told him to call on you [and] that you could do more for him in that part of Lauderdale and in Newton than any other man in that county. And if he should come down there I wish you would assist him some for I would like to see some of my old acquaintences from Mississippi. I could have went recruiting if I had wanted to, but I did not know whether there could be any recruits in that part of the state or not. And if I had went and failed in getting recruits, I never would have returned to my regiment.

Dear brother all I ask of you is to let everything lay so far as them damned rascals is concerned until I get home. And should they layway you or kill you, I swear and call up on my high heavens to witness that I will have revenge out of them. If peace is not made by the first of January, I will resign and come home. . . . From the news we have here now, the prospect for peace soon looks dull, but we do not know what will be done [because] we have no late news from Scott.

I must close. You must excuse bad spelling and mistakes as I am excited tonight. I must quit as it is now tatoo.

5. *Andrew Trussell to James Trussell, Buenavista, Mexico, November 21, 1847. TC, box 1, folder 3.*

Dear brother,

I enclose [for] you a newspaper published at Monterrey. My reason for enclosing it as a letter is that if I was to send it as a paper, as is commonly sent, it [would] never reach you. This paper has nothing of much importance to you. It has a song wrote by one of my friends belonging to the Texas Rangers. I have now news here that would be of any importance to you. One of our privates belonging to our regiment whipped a Virginia captain last Saturday and it has caused some little excitement in both regiments between the officers. But the Mississippians always wanted to fight when they are imposed on or mistreated. . . . General Taylor has gone home and old Wool has taken his place at Monterrey and has command of the [troops]. Colonel Hamtramic of the Virginia volunteers is in command of this post [and] he is no better liked than General Wool. . . .

6. *Andrew Trussell to James Trussell, Buenavista, Mexico, January 9, 1848. TC, box 1, folder 4.*

Dear brother,

. . . my health is much improved for the last four or five weeks. I have had a tolerable [but] tight time of it. The health of our company and regiment is very good at this time. The only disease now in the regiment is brought on by man's own imprudence. If it was not for that, our regiment would be in splendid health.

A report reached headquarters night before last that the Mexicans was raising troops at San Luis Potosí, Zacatecas, and Durango to advance on this line. Those states have always refused to furnish money or men as long as Santa Anna was at the head of the army. But now Santa Anna is under arrest [and] they offer to furnish fifty thousand troops and four million dollars to the support of the army provided that [Anastasio] Bustamente shall have command of the army. These states, with seven others, have always refused to take any part in the war because they was opposed to Santa Anna and called him a traitor. The above news was received from a Mexican newspaper published in San Luis Potosí and was brought by a Mexican spy that is in the employ of the United States. The papers further stated that they had 1,500 troops at the city of San Luis Potosí and that they had 1,200 at Zacatecas and Durango.

If this be the case, the 2nd Mississippi Regiment will have a showing yet. The boys are all in good spirits [and] they are anxious for a fight. It is reported here [that] we will go to [a] town about 120 miles from here by the [name] of Parras. I wish it was true, for we are very tired of this place. There is to be a soldier hung tomorrow at 10 o'clock for killing a Mexican in Saltillo on December 8th. He belongs to Captain Mer's company. It is a company made up of the Arkansas cavalry. After the battle at this place, there is only one company of them and they are called the Buena Vista Cavalry. They were the same company [that] shot [two men on] the 27th [of] December by order of court martial. They are, or were, both as brave as men as ever fought in Mexico and they both fought at Buena Vista. The [first] one that was shot told them when they went to shoot him that they was going to kill as brave a man as was in Mexico. They had to shoot him twice before they killed him. The first time, out of fifteen men, two hit him. Then they had to send them off and have more men detailed to shoot him. It was the Virginia and Carolinians that was detailed to shoot him. The order said [that] he must be shot to death by musketry and that let our regiment out and we was very glad. . . .

. . . yesterday we received the president's message here [on] the 29th [of] December. Every officer and soldier as far as I have heard who speaks of it is well pleased with his message. Orders has been received here to support the army off after the Mexicans. If this had been done twelve months ago, I think the war would have been closed before now. We do not expect to hear of peace until about Christmas. About that time I think I will get home.

I wrote to you that I would be at home some time this month, but it would not do for me to resign and go home. It would be too much joy for one man in our company and another thing [is that] the company is not willing for me to leave them. I had a little difficulty a few days ago. I stabbed a man in the shoulder but did not hurt him very bad. He is getting well [and] I was justifiable. His name was Cuen of Columbus, Mississippi. Captain Daniel stood to me like a man all through the difficulty . . .

we had a fine time here at Christmas. We had a fine fandango ball at Saltillo and there were some girls there as fine as I ever saw in the States. Some of the Mexican girls is very lively and rich too . . . good only knows when we will get home. We would be willing to volunteer for twelve months now.

7. Andrew Trussell to James Trussell, Buenavista, Mexico, February 28, 1848. TC, box 1, folder 4.

Dear brother,

. . . I am as heavy as I ever was in my life and I hope I will remain in good health while I remain in Mexico for I think I have had my share of sickness. Since I have been in Mexico, our company and regiment are in fine health. They is but three on the sick report for our company. One of them is R. N. Calhoun. He is to blame for his sickness [which] was caused by his own imprudence as many other cases in the regiment.

We are all in fine spirits tonight for we have orders to go to a town by the name of Mazapil, [Zacatecas] one hundred and forty miles southwest of here. There have never been any American troops there. They say [that] there is about 8 or 9,000 inhabitants there. The town is in one corner of the state of Durango near the corner of the state of San Luis Potosí and Zacatecas. The Mexicans there is and always has been opposed to peace and it is thought [that] we will have a little brush with the Mexicans there as there is but few of us. Our regiment and Captain Lewis's company of Texas Rangers is all that is going. Lewis's company is about 70 men strong [and] we are about 480 fighting men strong. General Wool gives us no artillery for he says [that] if we have to retreat, we can crop a mountain, which will cut off two days travel on foot and if we had cannon, we would have to leave it. For that reason, he thinks we had better go without it.

If we do not get a fight there, we never will have one in this country. I had the opportunity of coming home [to conduct] recruiting in the place of Steel, but we were ordered to Mazipil. And it is thought here by all the Mexicans, and Americans too, [that] we will have a fight when we get there. And [if] we do, I want to be with the company and for that reason. I refused to go home recruiting and I think peace will be made in [the] course of this year. And if it is, I don't want to travel the long road between here and home three times instead of one time. And if my regiment and company get into a fight, I want to be with them, for I want to have one fight. If we could get in one hard battle and I could come out safe, we then could return home with some honor. But if we never should get into a battle in one year, after we get home it never will be known that we had been in Mexico. I came here for a fight and I want it before I leave this country.

I expect, when the war closes, to go from here to California with a company that will be made up here from our regiment and the Texas Rangers. It is true, dear brother, that I often think of you and the balance of my connection and want to see all [of] you very bad. But it is out of my power to see you soon, if ever. But should I never get back, I would not be the first, brother. Thousands have died in Mexico fighting for the rights of their country. And I pray to die fighting to the death for the rights of my country. I had [just] as soon fight some of the damned tories in the United States as those yellow devils. Here I believe peace would [have] been made long ago if it had not been for some damn tories who call themselves Whigs. There are some honest Whigs in the army who say they are going to quit the Whig party when they return to the States. They say that they believe peace would have been made long ago if it had not been for some of the leading Whigs in the United States. The Mexicans think [that] if they can hold out until a new president is elected and if he is a tory, or I might say Whig, they can have peace on their own terms. For that reason, I think peace was not made long ago. I think those men will be looked upon in a few years as tories were in [17]76, for they are the same. . . .

Here we have had some fine frolicks with the Mexican señoritas. Ed [Davis] and myself was at a big Mexican wedding last night. Was a week ago we commenced dancing in the evening about 2 o'clock and danced until the next day until we were tired down and then we came to camp and stayed all night and next day we started and went to Agua Nueva and had another fandango ball and danced all night before we went to another fandango ball and had a fine time there. But Ed and myself is now parted for a while. The company of Rangers is sent to a town called Parras and we are going to Mazapil. . . .

8. *Andrew Trussell to James Trussell, Cedros, (state of Zacatecas), Mexico, May 5, 1848. TC, box 1, folder 4.*

Dear brother,

For three weeks past, until the last three or four days, we have been in fine spirits thinking that in a short time we would have the pleasure of shaking our old friends by the hands. But at present our feeling is quite different. The last advise we had from the Mexican congress is that there is no chance for peace. At one time, they only lacked ten or twelve members of having a quorum. The report is now that some of the members are going home. If this report is true, I have no reason to dispute it. It is a rather bad show for peace. It is not the intention of the Mexicans to make peace because they are, as a majority of them, doing better now than they ever did, for they can sell what they have to sell for four times as much as they could before the army came among them. And the Mexican that wants employment can get it from the Americans and get four times as much for it as they could from their own people. And a great many of them want to come under the laws of the United States. At every place on this line, where the troops have been stationed for some time, there is hardly a peon to be found. The Mexicans now can see that there is no chance for them to establish a republican government again. They can, or some of them can, see that Paredes intends to try and form a monarch government. If peace was now made with the United States, they would have war among themselves. They may talk of peace with Mexico, but there is more peace among them now than there would have been if the Americans were out of their country, for we are protecting them and their property from the Commanches.

I must here mention what a very rich old Mexican who lives near Parras said when Santa Anna sent for him to loan the government of Mexico two hundred thousand dollars to carry on with the war. The Mexican's name was don Amaniel. He was educated in the United States. He sent word back to Santa Anna that he could not loan it to the Mexican government. Santa Anna sent [word] back to him that if he did not loan it, that he would come down on him with his army [and] force him to loan the money. Don Amaniel sent word back to Santa Anna to come on as soon as he pleased, that General Taylor and General Wool were not far off. The above took place a short time after the battle of Buenavista. Don Amaniel is a very smart Mexican. He is now governor of the state of Coahuila. He wants that state annexed to the United States.

The Mexicans have occupied three positions since the war commenced. The first was to whip us off of the disputed territory of Texas. Next was to whip us out of their country. They failed [in] both of these positions. They now want the United States to overrun their country and take possession of all their country and annex it to the United [States]. This, I think, would not do for a great portion of the Mexicans are not capable of voting and they do not want [the] United States to make slaves of them. If they were entitled to vote, a few Mexicans here would control the presidential elections and all other elections in this country. They is men in this country that could control four or five thousand votes. I know two brothers that own three thousand peons and they could control their votes. For this and many other reasons too tedious to mention, it would not do for us to take them under our government. In short, the Mexicans are a bad looking race of people, they are at least two hundred years behind the time in everything, even fighting. You can see in their works, in the silver mines here that have been at work for a hundred years or more. They work them now as they did when they first commenced. They farm as the people did in [the] old times. Such people as those we have no use for under our government. I do not know what course our government will pursue. If the Mexican government does not ratify the treaty, I should not think it would do well at all for [us] to withdraw the troops to a line, as Mr. [Secretary of State] Calhoun and others propose. That, I should think, would not do for then we would have about fifteen hundred miles to garrison and a great part of the line would be very devient and would cost the government [a] large amount to keep supplies for the army and the twenty thousand troops [that] would be necessary for this line. Then the Mexicans could come and fight when they wished. We would then have to whip them again and we had [just] as well settle it now while we are here and have possession of the principal part of their country.

I would very well like it if they would relieve our regiment for I would like to see Mississippi one more time or see more of Mexico. If we could be in active service, I would not care for staying here one or two years longer. But to be here in garrison [with] nothing to do but drill and about every eight or ten [soldiers] may [have] guard duty to do. This I am tired of. I had much rather stayed at Buenavista, for we could have a fandango when ever we wanted to. But here the fools are afraid of us. It is only now and then that we can get up a fandango here. There is *one* American lady here, [and she is] Mr. Osborn, our beef contractor's wife. She is an old Texian. I was at her father's house when I was in Texas. I [had] become acquainted with her there but when I first saw her here, I did not know her. She made herself known to me. I stayed at her house a while when I was sick in Saltillo. She was as kind to me as if she had been my sister. It has been so long since I saw a pretty American woman that she looks to me to be the prettiest woman I ever saw. I would like to be in the United States to go to church one Sunday [and] to see the fine looking American girls and to see if they look as well as they used to look, although there are some fine looking Mexican señoritas here. This enough of my foolishness. . . . Texas Rangers will be disbanded in June.